D1234790

SINGLE WOMEN AND MONEY

SINGLE WOMEN AND MONEY

How to Live Well on Your Income

Margaret Price and Jill Gianola

ROWMAN & LITTLEFIELD
Lanham • Boulder • New York • London

Published by Rowman & Littlefield
An imprint of The Rowman & Littlefield Publishing Group, Inc.
4501 Forbes Boulevard, Suite 200, Lanham, Maryland 20706
www.rowman.com

86-90 Paul Street, London EC2A 4NE, United Kingdom

British Library Cataloguing in Publication Information Available

Library of Congress Cataloging-in-Publication Data

Names: Price, Margaret M., author. | Gianola, Jill, author.
Title: Single women and money : how to live well on your income /
    Margaret Price and Jill Gianola.
Description: Lanham : Rowman & Littlefield, [2021] | Includes bibliographical
    references and index. | Summary: "Single Women and Money addresses the
    financial concerns of all single women. With fresh solutions, the book tackles
    single women's deepest money fears. Readers, including widows, divorcees,
    and those who never married, get the tools needed to make their money
    last"—Provided by publisher.
Identifiers: LCCN 2021017406 (print) | LCCN 2021017407 (ebook) | ISBN
    9781538148570 (cloth ; alk. paper) | ISBN 9781538148587 (epub)
Subjects: LCSH: Women—United States—Finance, Personal. | Single
    women—United States—Economic conditions.
Classification: LCC HQ179 .P75 2021 (print) | LCC HQ179 (ebook) | DDC
    332.0240082—dc23
LC record available at https://lccn.loc.gov/2021017406
LC ebook record available at https://lccn.loc.gov/2021017407

∞™ The paper used in this publication meets the minimum requirements of
American National Standard for Information Sciences—Permanence of Paper
for Printed Library Materials, ANSI/NISO Z39.48-1992.

For America's 66 million single women

CONTENTS

ACKNOWLEDGMENTS

Where to start? So many people have generously contributed to the making of *Single Women and Money*. To them, we say a massive thank-you. This book would not have been possible without all their support and ideas.

A big shout-out to the many single women who shared their remarkable stories with us. Their unique experiences underscore the many rewards and challenges of being single in today's society.

Thank you to Marie Swift, who opened doors for us; John Willig, our agent; Suzanne Staszak-Silva, our editor, and the entire crew at Rowman & Littlefield.

We are grateful to Marlene Star and Mercedes Cardona for their professional contributions and to Jared Trexler and Meg Wannemacher for lending their expertise. Thanks, also, to Batya Yasgur for her editorial insights and to Diana Akhavan for her illustrations.

A big thank-you to the staff of Gianola Financial Planning, including Sana Haque, Melanie Dunbar, Kevan Murphy and Matthew Hofacre.

We also owe much to our family and friends; these patient souls have served as sounding boards as we wrote this book.

Above all, we thank Arthur Nealon and Dan Fleisch, our life partners, who listen, encourage and inspire.

PREFACE

It could be you—or your mother or daughter—trying to make ends meet as a single woman, often on one income, and typically earning less than men do. It can be a concern today and potentially a major problem tomorrow.

But society isn't paying heed. Even though women have marched in the streets about many vital issues, somehow the financial inequalities of single women haven't been front and center, haven't been blared from the megaphones. Few are clamoring for the changes needed to balance the scales and erase the single woman's disadvantage: surviving, often on one income, in a society focused on couples and dual-earning households.

Would these constraints disappear if single women would only wed? Does society still expect marriage to fix these inequities—as if that were always desirable or possible?

The fact is, many single women are being financially shortchanged, an overlooked reality that can affect them as young adults and potentially last into their old age.

Why should this disparity exist? And why should society let it continue? These issues spurred us to write *Single Women and Money*. We want to provide information to unmarried women whose financial needs have been overlooked. And we want to enlighten society about the financial needs of this large population.

In our chapters, we explore the financial issues—from saving and investing to making money last in retirement—most relevant to single women. And we delve into the ways these issues affect divorcees, widows and never-married women, specifically. There's also a chapter on where to find resources in hard times and a final chapter on how society can, and should, help single women.

We've strived to keep the information up to date. Because of our evolving economic and political landscape, though, some laws, policies or even data may have changed since we completed this book.

But overall, we hope this work will be an essential tool. It's not a tip sheet or a primrose path to fast profits or getting rich quick. It's a guide to how to make money last, hopefully through a long life. Although it is skewed to the interests of single women, we hope the book's messages will resonate throughout society and prompt needed changes. After all, why should single women be financially left behind?

INTRODUCTION

If you are an unmarried woman, you have plenty of company: in America, more than 66 million women are either widowed, divorced or never married.

And although some media portray you as fancy-free, reveling in the latest fashions or lounging at a chic beach resort, your reality may be different. Unlike dual-earning couples, you typically survive on one income and may scrimp on extras to cover your food, housing and transportation costs. Indeed, over your lifetime, you may pay more—by as much as $1 million—than married couples pay on taxes, health care and various other services. At least at times, you may have little cash available for Caribbean cruises.

There's also the pressure to save for the future. As a single woman, your financial safety net—the money you're able to save—has to stretch through your life. But will it last? What if a financial maelstrom were to suddenly sweep away assets, halving the value of your 401(k), as happened to some in the 2007–2009 market crash? Could you find your way back to solvency? What if a succession of crises were to strike, as happened to Christina Burruss?

Consider what Christina, a marketing professional, has endured—and overcome: wed in 2007, marital problems began early on for her amid infidelity by her husband who, she later learned, also was selling drugs. Eventually, tensions in the home exploded: in 2013, after her husband physically and verbally assaulted her, Christina and her children fled to her parents' house.

The problems didn't abate. During Christina's five-year divorce process, her spouse unsuccessfully battled her for custody of their children in order to get child support payments. And in 2019, she lost her 14-year job with an electronics company.

But Christina turned job loss into opportunity. In 2019, using funds from her severance package, she launched her own consulting firm specializing in brand and product marketing. It's fulfilling two of her goals: by working at home, Christina pursues her career while being home for her kids.

This story and others like it underscore some of the experiences of single women—their trials and triumphs and how they manage, often as solo earners. They typically support themselves and sometimes family members. Their numbers are legion and eventually could include women who are currently married. Indeed, it's possible that, amid the divorce rate and the demographics of longevity, all women will be single at some point as adults.

But many women aren't financially ready to live solo. Traditionally expected to marry and be supported by their spouse, many women have not been schooled in finance—at least not at home. According to a study by Allianz Life Insurance Company of North America, "fewer than one in five women, and only four percent of men, say they teach their daughters to be financially independent."[1]

That matters. This knowledge gap—this disadvantage for women—can stifle their ability to manage in a financial crisis and can worsen their fears about old age. Without a clear understanding of money—how to get it, grow it and make it last—women can face a lifetime of fears about outliving their funds.

Or if their savings are meager, they may believe that they can never retire.

Take the case of Alicia, from Northern California. She earned a master's degree and has had several careers over her adult life. But her salaries have never enabled her to save much money. Now in her 60s, Alicia works as a household helper to supplement her Social Security benefit. And she's unsure if, or when, she'll be able to retire.

And what about the deep-pocket crowd—those wealthy Americans who seem able to spend and luxuriate as they wish? Evidently, lack of financial knowledge can be frightening even for them. For instance, after the financial crisis of 2007–2009, one multimillionaire woman living in the South was so worried about misdeeds on Wall Street and potential market crashes that she feared "ending up as a bag lady on the street" if she gave her money to a broker. As a result, she kept her funds in cash, including some at home. That lasted until she finally consulted a financial advisor, who found better places for her money.

But maybe you aren't wealthy, financially strapped or afraid of investing. Instead, maybe you're simply wondering how to afford to buy a house and stop paying rent while still saddled with student loans. Or you are stressing over how to erase the balance on your high-interest credit cards. Or you're pondering one existential quandary: Who will care for you, and pay the bills, if you become incapacitated?

So what do you do? Are you ready to fend for yourself? Is there an amount of money that ensures you'll live comfortably?

To manage on your own, and perhaps support others, you need a guide to long-term financial security that's focused on your issues. The fact that you often survive on one income—which is typically less than what many men earn—strains your ability to save for the future. And if hit by a costly emergency, your savings may be depleted for years.

There is a path forward. *Single Women and Money* reveals the steps to take at every stage of life to lock in your financial security for the present and future. We provide fresh, clear solutions to such pressing questions as:

- How do I save for the future when I'm struggling to pay off debt?
- How do I avoid going broke in old age?
- How do I invest with confidence?
- What tax breaks can I take advantage of?
- What insurance do I need (*hint:* health and disability)?
- How do I find financial help in hard times?

Throughout the book, individual chapters zero in on issues and solutions and provide tools to help you chart your progress.

We'll discuss budgeting, spending patterns at different ages, investing, saving and breaking the cycle of debt. Although too few women have been educated about finance, we illustrate how some have figured out a key to successful money management: they identify and fund their priorities—their passions—and still stay within a budget.

Consider the examples of two single women: Karina Quintans, of Portsmouth, New Hampshire, and Russelyn Williams, of suburban Chicago.

Karina's passion is traveling, especially to developing countries. The self-employed woman affords these trips by using a "disciplined" approach to spending. But it wasn't always so. For a time during graduate school, she incurred significant student loan and credit card debt. That left her paying off the debt for years after grad school.

So Karina, currently a marketing and communications writer for government contractors, reassessed. She now spends on what's most important to her: travel and the ability to connect with distant cultures. By spending and saving to fit her values, Karina is now a homeowner and says she's "having an amazing life—free of debt."

For Russelyn, growing up in a household of seven people meant frugality. Because of limited income, her family shopped in thrift stores and at affordable grocers. Today, she gets a "modest" income as a homeownership counselor for South Suburban Housing Center, a counseling and fair housing agency certified by the US Department of Housing and Urban Development.

But the resilient Russelyn has not felt deprived. She financed college with scholarships and part-time work and, through her job, learned additional money management skills that she now teaches. Not only does she avoid overspending but she also proudly "purchase[s] below my means." Indeed, the condo she bought cost less than $100,000, even though she could afford something pricier. To fulfill her writing passion, she pumps money saved from "small sacrifices" into publishing and advertising her writing about women. And in 2021, her goal is to invest at least 15 percent of her income in a retirement fund.

Such stories—from personal interviews with women sharing their experiences—illustrate how it's possible to live the life you want. But challenges abound. What if you become unemployed? Can you land a good job even if you're over 55? If you're a parent, how do you find affordable childcare? And, ultimately, how do you ease the fears of running out of money in old age?

Single Women and Money tracks your needs at different ages and offers guidance separately to divorced, widowed and never-married women. We show you how to plan, how to build savings and make your money grow. If you're not investing, we show you how to jump in: how to start the process, how to assess your tolerance to risk and from there how to invest for the long term, typically in low-fee mutual funds. In addition, you'll discover safe ways to tap funds in retirement—including with a bond ladder—that enable you to avoid using up your savings.

And what about Social Security? This financial lifeblood for many retirees is dizzyingly complex, with rules and regulations thicker than some novels. But understand this system you must: the choices you make about Social Security—such as when to claim it and under what marital circumstances—can mean a difference of tens of thousands of dollars over your lifetime.

To help you navigate the Social Security maze, we answer such key questions as:

- When should you begin claiming Social Security to maximize its benefits?
- How much money can you expect to receive?
- What are the different rules that apply if you have never married, are divorced or are widowed?

Death and taxes are inevitable—and a special problem for singles. The unfair truth is that the unwed often pay comparatively higher taxes than married people do. We show you how to capitalize on any savings opportunities. And when it comes to estate planning, we direct you to what you need, including a will, a durable power of attorney, a living will and a health care power of attorney.

According to Caring.com's "2021 Wills and Estate Planning Study," only 32.9 percent of adults have a will.[2] But avoiding tough decisions around your estate planning—such as who will manage your affairs if you become incapacitated and to whom you should leave a bequest— have consequences. And they could affect your family.

Consider what happened to Catherine, who'd had little background in money management. Her husband, who died unexpectedly at age 57, left no will and no instructions for how he'd managed the family's money. As a result, his widow was left scrambling to figure out how to manage the household while the estate wound through the probate court process. Overwhelmed by the new and daunting tasks, Catherine lapsed into deep depression—until friends noticed her condition and stepped in to help.

How can you avoid this plight? What preparation gets you through life's uncertainties? Ultimately, how do you lay the groundwork for a financially secure life?

All this may seem ponderous—extra burdens heaped onto your already busy life—but it need not be. Whether you're working or retired, our book aims to demystify money issues. And we make it easy to get the answers you need as a single woman. If you're fretting over paying off your debt, chapter 6 will guide you. If you're worried about safeguarding your assets, flip to chapter 9. Or if you're lost in the labyrinth of the Social Security system, chapter 12 will light your path forward.

Ultimately, there's no reason to feel lost about money, because you don't need an MBA to be financially confident. And you don't need a spouse to pay the bills. What you need, in this age of women's empowerment, is information. It's here now. And it's tailored to your needs.

It's just gotten a whole lot easier to be single.

2

SINGLE WOMEN

How the Money Issues Vary

A "ring by spring." Honeymoon by June. These were once words for young women to live by as they were finishing up schooling. The idea, passed down like an heirloom, was to get and stay wed. Being married was the ticket to social and financial security.

But happily, such views now seem as quaint as laced-up corsets. With ever more options available today, women can now wed when they wish or not marry at all. And if they're not married, they have ample company: Today, almost half—49 percent—of America's females age 15 and older are unwed (versus 38 percent in 1970). Of today's single women, fully 61 percent have never married, 22 percent are divorced and 17 percent are widowed, per 2020 data of the US Bureau of the Census.

The women's stories are varied and compelling. Many have worked hard to support themselves and, in some cases, their family members. They've pursued careers and developed friendships. If widowed or divorced, they've fashioned new lives after the trauma of loss.

But however different their individual stories, these women share financial constraints: they often survive on one income. And like women overall, they typically earn less than the "typical" man. Their savings have to last through a potentially long life; yet financial strains leave many focused on how to pay the bills today.

What if their car dies, their home catches fire or their job disappears? Or the rent suddenly soars? Or a health insurer balks at paying a high medical bill?

How well can single women handle such unwelcome surprises? And which category of single women—widows, divorcees or those who never married—is most financially prepared?

Data from Fidelity Investments provide clues as to which group of single women is more advanced with regard to financial planning—and where more work is needed.

Among the findings in Fidelity's "Single Women & Money Study" is that, broadly, widows outscored the two other categories of single women on some key metrics. Among survey respondents, for instance, 56 percent of widows reported having a comprehensive financial plan versus 32 percent of divorced women and 17 percent of women who have never married.

Moreover, fully three-fourths of widows, versus 56 percent of divorcees and 46 percent of never-married women, had an emergency fund that would cover at least three to six months of their essential expenses. And as for estate planning? Data show widows with the commanding lead: 64 percent of those respondents had a plan in place versus 29 percent of divorcees and only 9 percent of women who never wed, according to the study.[1]

Why such disparities? Experts say factors such as women's age, income and experience with financial issues can all play a role. For instance, while married, some women may have engaged in financial and estate planning with their spouse.

But among the many women who weren't schooled in finance, this knowledge gap, this missing information about personal finance, could mean costly missteps, especially in a crisis—for instance, if a woman's assets suddenly shrank after a divorce or a never-married woman lost her job.

As this chapter illustrates, the social and financial issues, the risks single women face, differ by marital status—as do the recommendations for managing money and staying solvent.

IF YOU HAVE NEVER MARRIED

Happily, you're the boss of your own life—except perhaps at work. You can make your own choices and fashion the life you want. And only your income can cramp your style. But finances are often an issue. Typically, you rely on your own paycheck and may worry about unemployment or keeping clients. Although you're saving for a vacation, an emergency expense can grab those funds and waylay your plans. And over time—with each passing year—you may increasingly worry about the future: who will care for you in old age and how long your money will last.

As a solo earner, your job often takes center stage. "A job and career are very important, especially if a woman has no spouse, partner or children," observes psychotherapist Anstiss Agnew, who is also a child welfare expert. Beyond a paycheck, the job can provide a sense of satisfaction as well as a way to maintain social connections. Thus even if the work is tedious, women can enjoy being around, and bonding with, colleagues.

Additionally, jobs can provide money-saving benefits: possibly an employer-sponsored health insurance plan, a disability insurance plan or other group insurance offerings. Hopefully, the job will come with paid time off, including paid sick days and paid family leave. In addition, your employer may sponsor a retirement savings plan, such as a tax-advantaged 401(k) plan, which provides a convenient way to save for your future.

Even so, data show money issues weigh heavily. According to a 2019 survey commissioned by Fidelity, a staggering 92 percent of never-married women were stressed out about finances, versus 89 percent of divorcees and a lesser 65 percent of widows.

For all three groups of single women, paying monthly bills was the "most likely" contributor to the stress, the Fidelity survey showed. For never-married women, the second biggest contributor to the stress was "having enough money left over to enjoy day-to-day life, including socializing and entertainment," followed by concern about having enough funds to cover an emergency.[2]

Fortunately, Barbara, of Bronx, New York, can pay the bills. She'd had a rewarding 45-year nursing career, which enabled her to save

money, including through a 403(b) savings plan, and receive a pension
(as well as Social Security) at retirement. Along the way, she bought
a home in the Bronx—a five-bedroom, 100-year-old Victorian—and
a beach bungalow on Long Island, New York. While they were alive,
Barbara's parents shared her Bronx home with her and helped with
expenses.

These days, the retiree says that, although she can buy what she
wants, within reason, she is "careful about spending." Before making
any big-ticket purchases, like a new roof for her home, Barbara considers the urgency. Can it wait? If not, she determines how to pay for
it without racking up debt.

Key financial steps all never-married women should take:

☐ Create a budget—a plan for spending and saving. Then, track
  spending every month to ensure your outlays don't exceed your
  income.

☐ Ensure you have an emergency savings account that would cover,
  ideally, six months' worth of spending on necessities.

☐ As soon as possible, pay off high-interest debt, starting with unpaid credit card balances.

☐ Aim to save at least 15 percent of your income annually until you
  retire. Use tax-advantaged retirement plans, such as a 401(k), a
  403(b) or an Individual Retirement Account (IRA).

☐ Ask for promotions or salary increases at work as frequently as
  possible.

☐ If working, buy a disability insurance policy. Consider buying a
  long-term care insurance policy before age 60.

☐ Create an estate plan that includes a will, a financial power of attorney and a health care power of attorney, and update the plan
  as needed.

☐ Determine who—family members or others—will be your caregiver if you become disabled.

☐ By age 60 at the latest, determine when to retire and what retirement income you will receive. If possible, don't claim your Social
  Security benefit at least until you reach your full retirement age
  as defined by the Social Security Administration.

☐ Throughout life, prioritize discretionary spending to allow yourself the small, ongoing joys you cherish.

Linda Lingo, a California-based financial coach, describes how she finances desired extras: "I budget for beauty," says Linda. "Occasionally, I buy flowers for myself or, as needed, plants for my patio. The color and beauty I get from them are important to me." If this means forgoing some treat, such as dining in a restaurant, so be it; for Linda, the flowers take priority.

IF YOU ARE DIVORCED

If your marriage is on the skids or newly ended, you are likely to be awash in emotions. You may be feeling lost, angry and betrayed; you may be fearful of the future and wondering where you go from here. Or conversely, you may feel relief at this escape from a bad union.

If you've instigated the divorce, you have at least one advantage: "You've probably thought about leaving for a long time," holds Ginita Wall, cofounder and a director of the Women's Institute for Financial Education (WIFE).

But if you've been caught unawares—your spouse suddenly shocks you with the news that he's walking out—you feel like you've been bludgeoned.

As it happens, experts say more women file for divorce than men do. But however the breakup occurs—whichever spouse initiates it—divorce can be harrowing. Financially, both spouses are likely to take a hit, exiting their marriage with far fewer assets than they'd shared during the marriage.

How much of a financial loss can women expect? While that answer can vary with age, employment and other factors, data show a clear risk for older women. Consider the findings of a 2012 report by the US Government Accountability Office: "For women approaching, or in retirement, becoming divorced, widowed or unemployed had detrimental effects on their income security." With divorce, "women's household income on average fell 41 percent," which was almost twice the decline men experienced.

What's more, the breakup can introduce or worsen financial concerns. These fears can include managing alone and on a lower income, finding a job if you don't have one, paying off debt and planning for an uncertain future. If the divorce isn't amicable, you may be tempted to hasten the process—to "get it over with" by caving in on some demands. But don't do that, experts say: by accelerating the process, you could forfeit benefits you'll later need. "Some divorcees walk away with very little to their name because they were anxious to be done with the divorce process," observes Allison Alexander, a financial advisor and planner at Savant Wealth Management and a certified divorce financial analyst. She advises women going through divorce to seek help from a team of professionals—ideally including an attorney, a financial advisor, an insurance agent, a therapist and possibly a realtor. "The larger the bundle of support, the better a divorcee will do," she says.

The good news: over time, managing finances often gets easier for divorcees. Among the findings in a study by Allianz Life Insurance Company of North America, 62 percent of women divorced 10 years or more versus 44 percent of those divorced less than a decade said they had a "good" understanding of the financial products they owned, such as life insurance, annuities, stocks, bonds, education savings plans and 401(k)s and/or IRAs.

Moreover, 55 percent of those longer-term divorcees considered themselves "good" at saving for long-term goals, such as retirement, compared with 36 percent of those divorced for less than a decade, showed Allianz's "2019 Women, Money and Power Study."[3]

The following are key issues to address before, during and after a divorce:

- ☐ Before filing for divorce, become knowledgeable about your state's laws on alimony, child support and asset distribution.
- ☐ To limit the costs and acrimony of the divorce process, consider working with a mediator on your divorce settlement.
- ☐ Even when married, keep in your own name assets you've acquired or brought to the marriage, and have your own credit cards.

☐ When dividing assets, consult with a financial professional to ensure you receive a fair settlement and won't get hit later by a financial shock, such as a high tax bill from the sale of appreciated stock.

☐ If your spouse is awarded alimony from you, determine the most tax-advantaged method of paying it.

☐ Update your budget and your estate plan during, or immediately after, finalizing your divorce.

☐ Consider downsizing your home after divorce, especially if all your children are now adults.

☐ Maintain an emergency fund equal to six months' worth of spending on necessities.

☐ Determine whether you qualify for any of your ex-spouse's Social Security benefits. And, if possible, don't begin claiming your Social Security benefit before your full retirement age.

☐ If you're seeking a job after a hiatus from work, ensure your resume includes the skills you've acquired, or professional trends you've followed, while out of the workforce.

☐ Find additional sources of income that can last through your lifetime.

Consider how Kay Meyers, of Mukilteo, Washington, accomplished the last task on the list.

Years ago, while an employee at Boeing, Kay learned about the attractiveness of owning a self-storage business: not only could it provide a steady income from renters of its units but it could be managed by an otherwise retired person.

So, eventually, when Kay heard about a self-storage facility in foreclosure, she leaped at the chance to buy it. She obtained a bridge loan from the Boeing Employees' Credit Union (now BECU) to secure the mortgage for the self-storage facility, and she used some of her Apple Inc. stock as collateral for the bridge loan. In 2008, she worked with BECU again to refinance the mortgage loan so that she could expand the facility.

The moves have been rewarding. Kay's facility, called Mountainside Storage, has grown to 10 buildings with 275 storage units and has typically been fully rented. Today Kay collects Social Security, two pensions (from Boeing and from Reynolds Metals Co.) and rental income from Mountainside Storage. For her, Mountainside has been "a great source of steady income" (which she credits to her "A-Team" of managers).

IF YOU ARE A WIDOW

You're beset by grief and newfound loneliness. There's a sudden darkness worsened by fears of a future alone. How do you refashion a life previously built for two? How do you manage the household expenses alone? How do you even know which bills to pay?

These concerns piled on Susan, of Westchester County, New York, after her husband's sudden death from a heart attack. Since she had not been prepared for his passing, it created double misery: the loss of a loved one coupled with panic over how to maintain the household.

For others, there could be a long goodbye: months or even years spent caring for an increasingly ill spouse. Suspecting what lies ahead, a future widow can prepare financially and perhaps even emotionally. But doing so carries baggage: making preparations for life without the spouse can stir guilt—a sense that you've given up hope of the other's survival.

However, among single women, widows do have some advantages. "They get a lot of sympathy," observes Ginita Wall of WIFE. "There are grief and support groups for them, and churches reaching out"—more so to widows than to divorcees. "Some divorced women feel lonely because, for the most part, society doesn't have the same embrace for them."

Financially, various death benefits may accrue to widows. Payouts and other funding may include life insurance, a Social Security's survivor's benefit, survivor benefits in the late spouse's pension plan and inherited assets. As part of their 2018 study, "Widowhood and Money: Resiliency, Responsibility and Empowerment," Merrill Lynch and Age Wave found that 82 percent of widows (in this survey, "widows" refer to men and women who lost spouses) reported receiving "some sort of inflow of assets." Most commonly, this included a Social Security survivor's benefit, cited by 69 percent of respondents, and life insurance, received by 63 percent. According to the survey report, "the median amount that widows received from any of their spouses' accounts was $28,000."[4]

Of course, such payouts wouldn't begin to dent widows' grief. And in light of the ordeal these women face, they should avoid making major decisions immediately after the spouse's death. But the cold reality is that, on average, women outlive men. By boning up financially while married—participating in financial decisions, paying some household bills, discussing investments with their spouse—married women better prepare themselves, financially, for the possibility of someday living alone.

Key issues widows should address include:

- ☐ After the death of your spouse, contact your Social Security office to see whether you should apply for benefits under your work record or your late spouse's.
- ☐ Find out how much of your deceased spouse's employee benefits, such as a pension, you can obtain.
- ☐ Redo your budget, accounting for any changes to your income or liabilities. If you still have children at home, factor in their needs through college.
- ☐ Ensure that your budget includes provisions for medical costs, which are likely to rise as you age.
- ☐ Have an emergency fund to cover six months' worth of spending on necessities.
- ☐ Review your estate plan and beneficiaries of your retirement plans and life insurance policies to see if any changes are needed after the death of your spouse.
- ☐ Decide how to pay for long-term care costs, and set aside funds for this purpose if you don't have long-term care insurance.
- ☐ Continue, or take over, ongoing payments, such as utilities and repair costs. But avoid major financial decisions, such as whether to sell your house, for roughly a year after your spouse dies.
- ☐ Draw up a plan (or update an existing one) for withdrawing assets safely and systematically from retirement accounts.
- ☐ Identify a person who will be your caregiver if you become infirm.

By the time Elisa Robyn became a widow in 2016, her financial situation had long become secure. But it hadn't always been so. Early in her 29-year marriage, times were tough as Elisa struggled to find work while her husband's construction business waffled. During those darker days, the couple's bank account hit zero.

But eventually, the picture brightened: Elisa, who holds a PhD in educational psychology, landed a series of teaching and administrative positions at local colleges in Denver. Becoming the family's breadwinner, she earned steady income that eventually climbed to six figures. Her jobs also provided her with retirement benefits that included a pension.

Although shocked and grieved when her husband died of a stroke, Elisa was financially prepared. She had learned how to handle her own money—and was even ready to assist others. In 2019, she launched a consulting business that she says "helps people with their emotional relationship to money."

3

AGE MATTERS

As years go, 2020 was a doozy: a coronavirus pandemic struck, throwing society into a tailspin. Lockdowns ensued, businesses took a hit and social distancing became the norm. But Dr. Amanda Star, a chiropractor and Pilates instructor in Los Angeles, faced down the challenges.

In the spring of 2020, as the coronavirus raged, she produced several virtual healing programs for homebound clients. Later that spring, she got a plum offer, but securing it would take some work. Due to the pandemic, the owner of the physical therapy clinic where Amanda had been working decided to sell the business, and she pitched it to Amanda. Initially, the cost was too high. But over time, buyer and seller negotiated until the price became affordable. And on October 1, 2020, she took ownership of Align Physical Therapy & Chiropractic, in central Los Angeles. In short order, her patient list swelled at least 30 percent.

And this was just one year in the life of a young professional. Millennials such as Amanda can expect many life events and changes ahead, both personal and professional.

Consider the many divergent paths Susan Graham has traveled: she's moved from one coast to another and had two major careers, a marriage, a divorce and a net worth that catapulted from bare bones to seven figures.

In her 20s, the native of Queens, New York, began her career as a dental hygienist. She also taught dental hygiene as an adjunct professor at Columbia University. Married at age 31, she and her husband eventually moved to Connecticut and then to Michigan, where they divorced.

After teaching herself computer programming, Susan landed tech jobs that eventually brought her to Microsoft and its home state of Washington. It paid off: over the next six years, Susan amassed enough Microsoft stock options, through bonuses and purchases, to retire a millionaire at age 51. She next became an executive producer of a documentary film. And eventually, seeking broader social and cultural experiences, she moved to Southern California.

Such stories underscore how dramatically life can change: you may land a dream job and later lose it, obtain a job promotion that requires moving to a distant state, inherit a large property or find yourself suddenly and shockingly alone after the death of a spouse.

How do you manage, financially, with this unknowable future? The answer lies in charting a financial course, one that both maps what you expect your life to be and considers possible changes—the "what ifs" that could suddenly occur.

But how to design this map—this plan for spending and saving that can keep you on track? The process begins with creating a budget. Tailored to your financial needs, this process broadly defines how much to save and spend in various categories, such as food, clothing and shelter. You can adapt it to changing circumstances, such as a boost in pay or big-ticket purchases. Adhering to it can help you avoid mistakes that delay reaching your goals.

The spending/saving template below provides a guide. It reflects essential and discretionary spending, taking into account how much goods and services cost. As we will see, some of these recommended allotments for single women may not match their actual spending in various categories. But if generally followed, this guide can provide the basis for a lifelong spending plan.

THE IDEAL BUDGET

From after-tax (take-home) pay, you would spend:

- 30% for housing
- 15% for food
- 15% for transportation
- 12% for medical care and insurance
- 8% for apparel and related services
- 8% for entertainment and vacations
- 7% for debt repayment and savings for emergencies
- 5% for personal care

FUNDING FOR TAX-ADVANTAGED RETIREMENT ACCOUNTS

Contributions to a Roth IRA come from after-tax income. To fund a Roth IRA, use money from any bonuses or reduce spending on discretionary items such as personal care or vacations.

Contributions to retirement savings plans, such as many 401(k)s or traditional Individual Retirement Accounts (IRAs)—as well as premiums paid for your employer's health insurance plan—are deducted from pre-tax income. Aim to designate 15 percent of that pre-tax pay to your retirement plan, especially if you are age 40 or older. If self-employed, aim to save between 10 percent and 15 percent of your profits in a Simplified Employee Pension (SEP) IRA, which is a retirement plan geared to business owners and the self-employed.

SINGLE WOMEN'S *ACTUAL* EXPENDITURES

The above guide aims to address current and future needs. But does it reflect reality—how much single women actually spend? Does it meet the needs of single women living on a solo income? Will the 30 percent housing allotment work in large urban areas? At what ages are women most likely to be overspending?

Bureau of Labor Statistics (BLS) data provide illuminating information on single women's actual earnings and spending. The BLS's
Consumer Expenditure Survey for 2018–2019 of single women's expenditures tracks their average outlays during that period in a range
of categories and at different age groups. The survey also covers single
women's average earnings both in total and at different age brackets.
The data enable women to see where their spending goes, on average,
and how it may change in future years.

Selected data from the BLS survey:

Income. In the same report, single women across all ages (16 and
older) had an average annual income of $33,057 before taxes and an
estimated $29,206 after taxes. (Single women's after-tax income was
a whopping 32.8 percent less than the estimated after-tax income of
single males, according to the BLS's comparable study of single men.)
In the 2018–2019 period, single women's average after-tax earnings—
the money they can use for spending—climbed from a low of $13,365
for single females under age 25 (but at least age 16) to a peak $44,272
for those ages 35 to 44, sliding to $25,306 among those age 65 and
older. (The BLS data are all average annual amounts.)

Expenditures. Spending patterns varied with age. But across all
age brackets studied, the three most costly outlays—housing, transportation and food—devoured fully 79 percent of all single women's
after-tax earnings, according to the BLS's 2018–2019 statistics (figure
3.1).[1]

The housing bite. Housing and related costs alone, such as utilities, furnishings and the like, swallowed 48 percent of single women's
after-tax income. But among two age groups, single women 65-plus
and those younger than 25, housing costs absorbed more than 50
percent of income. And even for the highest earning group of single
females—those ages 35 to 44—shelter and related costs consumed a
breathtaking 42 percent of take-home pay, the BLS data show (figure
3.2).

Until middle age—in this case, starting with the 55-to-64 age
group—single women spend more on rented, than owned, homes, the
BLS data show. (As expenses for owned dwellings, the BLS includes
mortgage interest and charges, property taxes and maintenance, repairs, insurance and other costs.)

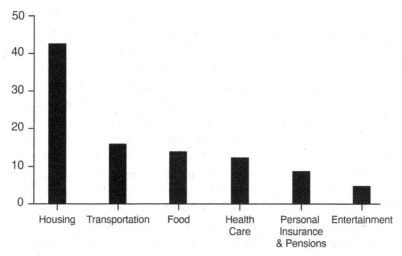

Figure 3.1. Categories of Highest Spending by Single Women as a Percent of Their After-Tax Income, 2018–2019. *Source:* US Bureau of Labor Statistics report.

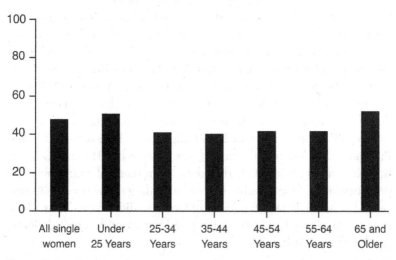

Figure 3.2. Housing Outlays by Single Women as a Percent of Their After-Tax Income at Different Ages, 2018–2019. *Source:* US Bureau of Labor Statistics report.

However, home ownership is evidently enticing. "Single females are second only to married couples when it comes to buying homes," reports Jessica Lautz, vice president, demographics and behavioral insights at the National Association of Realtors (NAR). She cites a strong desire among single females "to have a place to call your own."

Most commonly, single women buy detached single-family homes, followed by townhouses. In fact, they purchase townhouses or condos at a higher rate than single males or married couples do.[2] And often, she says, these women intend for their home to be multigenerational.

To afford a home purchase, 39 percent of single women made sacrifices in the year ending June 2020, according to NAR's report titled *2020 Profile of Home Buyers and Sellers*. Most often, this entailed less spending on luxuries and nonessentials, entertainment and clothes. Among other belt-tightening moves, some single women canceled vacations, took a second job or temporarily moved in with family or friends.[3]

But whether they're renters or homeowners, single women are typically devoting a huge chunk of income to housing. That, along with outlays for other essentials, can leave a relative pittance for such extras as personal care and entertainment, data show.

And evidently, planning and saving for retirement can get short shrift, especially by younger people. "For some of these people, retirement seems years away. They're more focused on dealing with their current monthly or annual expenses," explains Geoffrey Brown, CEO of the National Association of Personal Financial Advisors (NAPFA). "In addition, some of them may have lived through several economic downturns" and observed their impact on the markets and savings.

A NAPFA survey taken in 2019 underscores these points. It found that more than half of millennials (ages 23 to 38 in 2019) and Generation Xers (ages 39 to 54) hadn't done retirement planning over the prior two years. One possible upshot: according to the survey, 30 percent of millennials and 36 percent of GenXers didn't know if, or when, they could ever retire.[4] (The survey did not identify respondents by gender or marital status.)

HOW TO MAKE IT WORK

The bottom line on income and outlays: they don't match. Across all adult age groups, the BLS's 2018–2019 data on single women show they spent more than they earned—by an overall average annual 23 percent. But amounts of red ink varied: while overspending was most pronounced among the low-earning "under 25 group," data show that the highest earners, those in the 35-to-44 age bracket, overspent by a comparatively modest 3 percent.

What can be done? How can single women make ends meet while slogging through financial crises, family upheavals, illnesses and salaries that have typically fallen short of men's?

Eileen figured it out. Married at age 21, the New Yorker separated from her physically and verbally abusive husband at age 29 and eventually divorced him. While married, she had two children, including a son who is autistic. To raise the children without a penny of support from her estranged husband, she worked three part-time jobs. Over those years, Eileen's low wages—she lacked a college degree—covered her household and children's expenses but left nothing for her needs.

But eventually, the picture brightened: While working part-time in customer service at a company called Teleprompter Corp., officials noticed Eileen's talent at interacting with the public. That earned her a full-time job at the cable company and, from there, ongoing promotions. Surviving mergers, buyouts and layoffs, Eileen rose to the ranks of a department manager. By the time she retired in 2012, from a company by then known as Time Warner Cable, she was pulling in $145,000 a year. It was light-years from her $4.85 an hour starting wages at Teleprompter.

The takeaway: perseverance is rewarding, and showing initiative pays off. Experts say more women should follow suit. To gain visibility in an organization, they should speak up: suggest ways to boost business, volunteer for assignments and ask for promotions and pay raises.

And as for spending? Consider your short- and long-term needs and goals. From there, determine what you need now, what you can postpone buying and which tempting purchases to pass up.

But remember to treat yourself periodically—without falling into debt.

KEY STEPS AT DIFFERENT AGES

Over each decade of your life, you'll face different financial issues. Potentially, these range from paying off student loans as a young worker to affording medical care in retirement. Here are specific actions to help you stay solvent:

In your 20s. There's a lot to consider as you begin your career. Start by creating a budget to address the many new expenses you're facing. Tally your essential costs, such as housing, transportation, food, clothing, debt repayment and some savings. If that total exceeds your take-home pay or leaves peanuts for personal spending, figure out what you can trim. For help with budgeting, visit websites such as Mint.com or YNAB (www.youneedabudget.com).

To save on housing, which is likely your biggest expense, consider sharing space with a roommate. Or live with your parents for a time. If such moves won't trim your rent bill to a maximum 40 percent of take-home pay (better yet, 30 percent), think about relocating to a lower-cost community.

In the transportation area, travel on buses, subways or trains to avoid the costs of buying and maintaining a car, or share rides to work. If shopping for a car, consider a late-model used one, and plan to keep it at least six years.

Fully use your employee benefits. These can range from health insurance and possibly other coverage, such as disability, to stock options, access to emergency funds and, in some cases, use of a company car and even subsidized housing.

If your employer offers a retirement savings plan, such as a 401(k), 403(b) or 457, sign up for it unless you're automatically enrolled when you join the firm. If your company offers matching contributions (puts a percent of your salary into the account), take full advantage of the match: Contribute at least the same percent your employer matches, say, 6 percent of your pre-tax wages. If you have no access to an employer-sponsored retirement plan, create an IRA and have it automatically funded from your checking account after each pay period. When you're starting out in your career, aim to put at least 5 percent to 6 percent of pre-tax wages into your retirement account. By your 40s, plan to be contributing 15 percent of your income. In these years when you may not be earning top dollar, find out whether you qualify for certain tax credits, such as the Retirement Savings Credit. Such credits are subtracted from your federal income tax.

In your 30s. Save for big-ticket items, such as a down payment on a house, mortgage payments and furniture costs. But don't get too extravagant: Even though your income is likely to be growing, aim to keep housing costs as close as possible to your 30 percent target. If it runs higher, look for cuts among discretionary items, such as a vacation and personal care.

Seek ways to further boost income—from requesting a raise as often as you think prudent to working extra hours to taking a second job. And if you prefer self-employment, take a cue from Dr. Amanda Star: aim for a career with prospects for steady, long-term income growth.

If you have children, buy term life insurance for yourself, and ensure that your health insurance policy covers everyone you're responsible for. Aim to contribute at least 10 percent of your gross pay to a retirement savings plan. At your age, invest at least 60 percent of those retirement funds in stocks for long-term savings growth.

In your 40s. Review your spending. If you have children, factor their educational costs into your budget without paring back your savings for retirement. Hopefully, by this point, you've repaid any student loan debt and fully funded your emergency spending account. If so, shift those budget allocations, of 5 percent of net income each, to other spending needs, such as housing costs—or a much-needed vacation.

By this time, ensure that you're steadily contributing to your retirement account.

In your 50s. If you're short on retirement funds, play catch up. Starting at age 50, you can contribute amounts that exceed the general contribution caps to tax-advantaged retirement plans. (For example, in 2021, people age 50 and older can put an extra $6,500 into their company's retirement plan beyond the $19,500 limit.)

Bone up on payout options of your retirement plan, and by this age, obtain a long-term care insurance policy, if possible, from your employer.

Don't feel you have to pay off your mortgage yet. Since mortgage interest rates are generally lower than average earnings on investments, prioritize saving for retirement over paying off the mortgage.

If divorcing, consult with professionals, such as a financial planner and/or your attorney. They can explain the financial impact of choices you may be considering and—although there are no guarantees— help you maximize the settlement you get, advises financial planner Lori Lustberg of Pathway Financial Advisors.

Be sure your estate plan is in order, including your last will and testament, durable financial power of attorney and health care directive, and that you have named beneficiaries of your accounts.

In your 60s. Create or review your retirement spending strategy. Compute how much you will be able to tap your retirement savings every year without eventually going broke. Understand your Social Security benefits, including provisions for widows and divorcees, and if possible, avoid claiming your Social Security benefit until age 70, when you'll receive the maximum benefit.

Factor rising health costs into your budget: According to the BLS, single women ages 65 and older pay almost 19 percent of after-tax income for health care. If you think medical costs will be a squeeze, consider keeping your job for few more years to gain income and to remain on your employer's health insurance plan.

If you're newly widowed, take time to grieve and avoid hasty decisions, says advisor Lori Lustberg. An action plan she recommends: after the first three months of widowhood, begin evaluating your finances with modest steps, such as examining your income and expenses; after six months, review your investment portfolio for any desired changes; and, after a year, start longer-term planning, such as where you want to live.

In your 70s and beyond. At age 72, you have to start taking required minimum distributions from your tax-deferred (non-Roth) retirement plans. But if that income and any other, such as Social Security payments and any pension, still leave you short, consider applying for a reverse mortgage on your house or taking a part-time job. Cut costs by downsizing your home and keeping eyes peeled for senior shopping days and discounts.

And, if need be, seek assistance from the array of social programs that benefit seniors. Among the possibilities: Medicaid, property tax relief, food programs and home energy assistance. As Cindy Hounsell, president of the Women's Institute for a Secure Retirement (WISER), stresses, "Take advantage of government programs that can help."

4

SINGLE MOTHERS

If you've ever wanted to be a pro juggler, try being a single mom. You cook meals for the family, look after the children and take them to doctors when they're sick. You attend parent-teacher sessions and the kids' sports events. And, somehow, magically, with all the pins you've got flying in the air, you hold down a job. You love the mommy role and wouldn't trade it for anything.

But it's expensive, nonstop and sometimes emotionally grueling. You make sacrifices to create a warm, loving home. And you wish you could do more for the family. But money can be tight, especially if you're footing all the bills on your one income.

Of course, many others share your joys and challenges. According to 2020 data of the US Census Bureau, more than one-fifth—21 percent—of America's children under age 18 live with their mother as the solo parent in the household.

Of those children, almost half—49.3 percent—live with a mom who has never married. Another 28.9 percent of these children reside with a divorced mother, while 12.5 percent live with a mother who is separated, 3.9 percent live with a widow and 5.4 percent reside with a married mother whose spouse is absent, census data show.

For many of the moms, expenses can seem mountainous. While housing, food and childcare/education claim the biggest chunk of a single mother's budget, according to the US Department of Agriculture (USDA), the spending hardly ends there: from diapers to prom wear, and from sandboxes to baseball camp, the list of outlays can seem endless.

Consider this: it will cost a single parent an estimated $172,200 to raise a child born in 2015 through age 17, according to the report "Expenditures on Children by Families, 2015," by the USDA's Center for Nutrition Policy and Promotion. (Data are for single-parent families with before-tax income of less than $59,200 in 2015 dollars. Expenditures reflect the US average for the younger child in a two-child family.)

Of course, having money helps. But many single moms aren't well-to-do—or even earning an equitable wage. Indeed, "in the US being a mother is a greater predictor of wage discrimination than being a woman," holds Kristin Rowe-Finkbeiner, executive director and CEO of MomsRising (www.momsrising.org), an organization with more than a million members that advocates for mothers and families. As her organization illustrates, mothers in the United States overall typically earn 70 cents for every dollar paid to dads. And people of color have it worse: for every dollar paid to white, non-Hispanic dads in this country, Black moms typically earn 50 cents; Native moms, 47 cents; Latinx moms, 45 cents; white moms, 69 cents; and Asian American Pacific Islander moms, 89 cents.[1]

And pay inequity is just one problem. Other major financial concerns range from lack of child support payments to joblessness.

Data of the Census Bureau show how unreliable child support payments can be. In its report "Custodial Mothers and Fathers and Their Child Support: 2015," the Census Bureau revealed that 69.3 percent of custodial parents who were owed child support received some payments from noncustodial parents. But only 43.5 percent reported obtaining the full amount they were due.

In turn, joblessness can be especially dire for mothers who support their family on their solo income.

But for single moms, working can create another set of problems, as occurred during the coronavirus pandemic. In 2020, as the pandemic whipsawed the economy, triggering widespread job losses and shuttering schools and childcare facilities, single moms who were able to stay employed faced a horrific dilemma: How to care for their children who were now home during the day instead of at school or in day care? Although quitting work was one solution, it raised an existential question: Who would support the family if the single mother—the family's breadwinner—wasn't employed?

This crisis, which dragged on into 2021, highlighted just some of the challenges of raising children while holding a job. But for many single moms, the hurdles and challenges are ongoing as they grapple with family and work responsibilities amid an ever-uncertain economy.

Fortunately, single mom Tisha Tyler has managed, and remained resilient, through many economic ups and downs.

For several years after her first child was born, Tisha was a stay-at-home mom and the wife of a pastor. But after her husband was ousted from his congregation for conflicts with church officials, he fled his family and the state of California, prompting Tisha to become the family's breadwinner.

She quickly rose to the task and, over time, built a career in marketing. Along the way, she earned promotions and commendations and an MBA degree. But invariably, she'd face setbacks: the jobs would fall prey to toxic work environments, cutbacks or office closures. "At one point, I went from a $100,000-a-year job to food stamps and public assistance," Tisha recalls. Through it all, however, she ensured that her kids, now successful adults, would get the best schooling possible.

Eventually, Tisha moved to Maryland, where she founded a consulting firm focused on helping firms undergoing a transition. In conjunction with that business, she has been penning a three-book series that describes ways to shed the emotional blockages that prevent people from achieving their goals. The books partly borrow from Tisha's own story of triumphs and pain.

For Tisha, raising children has been an "honor" and well worth the stress and worries. But for moms, there's also a lot to think about—including expenses that some mothers might not be considering.

EXTRA COSTS FOR SINGLE MOMS

Beyond providing for basic necessities and, hopefully, some family fun, expenses also should include outlays for protecting children if something happens to you. And of course, there's the cost of child-care, which can empty your wallet.

Financial Protections

Since you can't predict what could happen to you, you need to financially and legally protect your kids at least as soon as they are born. What if you became incapacitated or you died? Who would care for your children and ensure they were raised as you'd have wanted? Who would pay their costs?

To safeguard your children, you need to take two crucial financial protections: create an estate plan that includes your will, and obtain life insurance on yourself.

The steps can work as a package: life insurance would provide money (a "death benefit") to support the children if you die; in turn, a will would dictate both how to distribute your estate upon your passing and who would become the guardians for your children.

Creating a will need not be expensive. If your finances and/or family structure aren't complicated, you can use an online service for relatively low or perhaps no cost. However, if your finances or family arrangements (such as having a bevy of stepchildren) are far-flung or complex, you'd be wise to seek help from an attorney.

With life insurance, keep the following in mind:

- You'd want "term" life insurance—meaning that the coverage expires at a set date. Common terms include 10, 15, 20 and 30 years. When considering the amount of your policy's death benefit—the payout to beneficiaries after you die—aim for a benefit equal to roughly 10 times your annual pre-tax income.
- Be sure to designate beneficiaries.
- If you die and your minor children are the beneficiaries, they cannot receive the policy's death benefit directly until they reach the age of majority. To address this issue, name a financial cus-

todian or trust. That person or entity would hold death benefit funds for the kids until they became adults. If you die while your children are still minors, the payout would go to the trust or the custodian (who could be the guardian you've named in your will) whom you've designated as the beneficiary.

To find a policy, start by exploring whether your employer offers life insurance as a benefit. According to a 2018 report by LIMRA, a research trade association for the financial services industry, 48 percent of private sector employers offered life insurance to workers in 2017. Of those that did offer it, 46 percent paid 100 percent of the premium, while 41 percent paid between 10 percent and 90 percent of the premium.[2]

You also can buy a life insurance policy on your own. Consider this option if you expect to change jobs during your career. You can find insurers easily through the internet and estimate how much insurance you need through such sites as www.dinkytown.net.

Health Coverage

Health insurance is another must-have. Be sure your plan covers your kids unless they are included in your ex-spouse's plan. Data show that many Americans obtain their health insurance through their workplace. If your plan covers children, they can stay on it, in most cases, until age 26. But if you don't have job-based insurance, consider obtaining coverage through the Health Insurance Marketplace, at www.HealthCare.gov. If you no longer have group health insurance because you're working reduced hours or you quit or lost your job, in many cases, you can continue the group health coverage for a limited time through COBRA (the Consolidated Omnibus Budget Reconciliation Act), and you would pay the full insurance premium. If you don't want COBRA coverage, which can be pricey, consider enrolling in a plan through the Health Insurance Marketplace (HIM).

Indeed, the 2021 passage of the American Rescue Plan made premiums on HIM policies much more affordable at least temporarily. Consider: during tax years 2021 and 2022, even if you earn more than four times the federal poverty line (which is $17,420 a year for a family of two), you won't have to pay more than 8.6 percent of your income for a HIM policy.

Other health coverage options include Medicaid, which is a public health insurance program for low-income families, children, pregnant women, the elderly and people with disabilities; and the Children's Health Insurance Program, known as CHIP. The latter provides health insurance to children in families with income too high to qualify for Medicaid but low enough to make private health insurance unaffordable. The children need to be younger than 19 and not covered by a group health plan. (For details on CHIP, visit www.HealthCare.gov or www.medicaid.gov.)

Childcare

If you're a working single mother, you typically need day (or night) care for the kids. But finding reliable, quality care can be arduous, and the cost of it can be out of reach. For help finding childcare providers in your state, start by visiting the government's website, ChildCare.gov, and clicking "Find Child Care." In addition to this tool, the site provides a wealth of information on such topics as childcare options, tips for choosing providers and ways to pay for childcare.

As for care costs: expect to pay a bundle. As a national average, in 2019, day-care centers charged $11,346 a year for full-time care for an infant and $20,414 for an infant and a four-year-old. At family-care centers, costs averaged $9,106 for the full-time care of an infant and $17,483 for an infant and a four-year-old, according to data from Child Care Aware of America (CCAOA).[3]

The US government recommends that families spend no more than 7 percent of household income on childcare. But, evidently, single moms may pay much more, depending on the type of care as well as the frequency of its use and any subsidies obtained. According to CCAOA, at a day-care center in 2019, median-income single mothers would spend, on average—without any government aid—42 percent of annual income for full-time care of an infant and a whopping average 75 percent of income for full-time care of an infant and a four-year-old. At a family-care center based in a home, the moms would pay an average 33 percent of income for full-time care of an infant and an average 64 percent for an infant and a four-year-old.[4]

Concludes Kristina Haynie, CCAOA's senior data analyst: "Center-based care is very unaffordable. Even with financial subsidies paying some of the cost, it would be out of reach for many single mothers."

Facing such sticker shock, many parents use multiple types of childcare, some of which are free or low cost. In fact, 63 percent of all kids younger than age five spend at least part of a week with a relative, according to "Working Families Are Spending Big Money on Child Care," a 2019 report by Rasheed Malik, senior policy analyst at the Center for American Progress. Indeed, almost 45 percent of all young children spend some time in the care of a grandparent, Rasheed's report shows.[5]

Even so, costs are still substantial, especially for single moms. Even when combining free and paid care, mothers who are divorced, separated or widowed spend an average 15 percent of their income on the care of kids younger than five—more than twice the government's recommended outlay. Never-married moms spend an even higher average 23 percent of income for care of children younger than five, according to Rasheed Malik's 2019 study.[6]

Cutting Costs   So how do you ease some of the financial burden of childcare? Options can range from help provided by family members or friends to government programs to employee benefits. Start by exploring any employee benefits. Some possibilities could include on-site childcare, flexible working hours, job-sharing or working from home. To save on taxes, see if you qualify for the federal Child Tax Credit as well as the Child and Dependent Care Tax Credit; both are detailed in chapter 10.

And if it's offered at work, also consider setting up a Dependent Care Flexible Spending Account (FSA). (Although tax provisions have been changing, this account could be an alternative to taking the Child and Dependent Care Tax Credit.) With a tax-advantaged FSA, your company can deduct a specified pre-tax amount per year—up to $10,500 in 2021—from your salary to pay for the care of children under age 13 and adult dependents needing care. With this account, you first pay out of pocket for such eligible expenses as preschool, summer day camp and eldercare, among others, and then get reimbursed.

In the spring of 2021, President Joe Biden proposed more assistance to families struggling to afford childcare. Among the provisions of his American Families Plan, low- and middle-income families would pay no more than 7 percent of their income on high-quality childcare.

Among the existing programs for those with low-income is the Child Care and Development Fund (CCDF). That federally funded program provides grants to states to help low-income families pay for childcare because of parents' need to work, attend school or participate in job training. To see if you qualify, visit www.benefits.gov /benefit/615.

In addition, the federal Head Start program promotes school readiness for children in low-income families. Begun in 1965, the program provides educational, nutritional, health and other services. While Head Start serves children ages three to five, Early Head Start is available to qualified infants, toddlers and pregnant women. To find a program, use the Head Start program locator at https://eclkc.ohs.acf .hhs.gov/center-locator.

Outreach and Support   To be sure, many moms turn to family, friends and neighbors for help with childcare. Some mothers set up nanny-sharing arrangements or "childcare swapping," the latter involving moms taking turns watching each other's kids.

But money isn't the only issue. Beyond the costs of child-rearing, there are the stresses—physical and emotional—of managing a job and household as a single parent without the support of a partner at home. With this "big picture" in mind, some single mothers have adopted broad approaches to helping themselves and other single moms through networks and communities. One such example is the organization, Single Mothers by Choice (www.singlemothersby choice.org), founded by Jane Mattes.

When her son was born in 1980, Jane was fortunate: her mother retired from her job to help Jane, who had become unexpectedly pregnant and planned to keep her child. As arranged, her mother would babysit while Jane, a New York City psychotherapist, was seeing patients.

But child-rearing required more help and support. In 1981, in a meeting in her living room with several other single moms, Jane organized the support group that became Single Mothers by Choice. Today, this network for single mothers has roughly 30,000 members and chapters in some 30 US and Canadian cities. Many members have children through donor insemination, since, as Jane explains, the women "want to be mothers before their biological clock runs out." They take this path "knowing that, at least at the onset, they will be parenting alone."

Members can connect online or in person, sharing concerns, information and ideas. Issues can be virtually anything related to moms. But there's one ever-pressing topic, even for this group whose average income runs close to $100,000 a year: the cost and availability of quality childcare. "Childcare," as Jane points out, "is a huge expense unless you're lucky enough to have parents who can help."

The Motherful Model   But what if single moms want something even more expansive: a single program that addresses a multitude of needs, is located close to—or where—the mothers live and is always accessible?

In 2018, those ideas prompted Heidi Howes of Columbus, Ohio, and two friends to create Motherful (www.motherful.org), an organization with a comprehensive view on how to support single moms. To Heidi, it's akin to a kibbutz.

The concept arose partly from Heidi's experiences as a divorced mom. After her marriage ended in 2010, she became overwhelmed by the tasks of work, running a household and raising two children, one of whom became severely ill. After fatigue and stress left Heidi nearly immobilized, her mother came from out of state to assist her. Eventually, friends recommended acupuncture and chiropractic services, which helped Heidi recover.

But the message had been driven home to Heidi that single moms shouldn't try to do it all alone. With that concept, Motherful began, initially with community dinners for single moms and their children. The organization subsequently expanded to include a communal garden, food pantry and an emergency fund that provides grants for members of up to $250.

At this writing, even bigger plans are in the works: within several years, the group hopes to provide a housing complex for single moms and their kids. Funded through a capital campaign, this "intentional community" ideally would include on-site childcare, a playground, gardens, a shared kitchen and even homeschooling for mothers who want that option for their kids.

"It isn't feasible for one parent to do it all," says Heidi, Motherful's executive director as well as cofounder. "We need a village. So that's why we're creating this paradigm for parenting."

5

GETTING A JOB—ESPECIALLY AFTER AGE 55

Unless you are a trust-fund baby or lottery winner, your income comes from working for a living. So until you retire, that means having a job.

But how do you find one if you're 55 or older, especially if you're competing against a large crop of younger, perhaps tech-savvier people? Or you've been absent from the workplace for a time due to unemployment or family demands? Or your occupation has gone the way of the town crier?

Of course, you could start your own business.

But if you're angling for a job with a predictable salary and some benefits—which has advantages, if you depend on your own earnings—it can be tough landing a job with an employer, especially for older women. Lingering ageism and sexism can further steepen the climb to the top of the applicant pack.

Despite the Age Discrimination Act of 1967, ageism is evidently still alive and well in the workplace. And the male-female wage gap provides just one measure of it: according to a 2020 report by the National Women's Law Center, women ages 45 to 64 working full-time year-round typically earn 76 cents for every dollar their male counterparts make. For working women age 65 and above, the figure is 81 cents.[1]

But don't let those numbers get you down. With groups such as Old School, CoveyClub and AARP, support and resources have been growing for older women who want to work. Many organizations are pushing back against attitudes that make it harder for older workers to get and stay employed. They can make strong arguments: among their many draws, older workers need limited training for a job in their field, and often, they've built a wide network of business contacts that they'd bring to a new job.

To be sure, events surrounding the coronavirus pandemic—the recession and joblessness—pounded some women-friendly sectors such as retail and hospitality. But the pandemic also spotlighted pressing needs, as well as long-term opportunities, especially in health care and related fields.

Indeed, the whole area of health and healing—telehealth, mental health counseling and others—offers abundant opportunities for women, says Lesley Jane Seymour, CEO of CoveyClub, a community for women 40-plus.

In a press release covering its "Employment Projections: 2019–2029," the Bureau of Labor Statistics (BLS) reported the occupational groups "in which employment is projected to grow markedly faster than the average" included health-care support occupations, community and social service occupations, and computer and mathematical occupations. (However, the 2019–2029 projections did not reflect the impact of the COVID-19 pandemic and response efforts, the BLS stated.)

The projections are the basis of the BLS *Occupational Outlook Handbook*. Among the *Handbook*'s alluring information: occupations the BLS projects to grow "much faster than average"—with 2019 median pay of $80,000 or more—include financial managers, health specialties, teachers (postsecondary), management analysts, medical and health services managers, nurse practitioners, software developers and software quality assurance analysts and testers.

So how do you find and land opportunities? The key lies in knowing what you want and from there determining how your talents, experience, personality and even contacts will get you the job. Determine why you're "the one" for the job you have in mind, and then go after it, advises Bonnie Marcus, an executive coach and author of the book *Not Done Yet! How Women over 50 Regain Their Confidence and Claim Workplace Power*.[2]

The major elements of your job-hunting campaign include: a resume that highlights your achievements; outreach that includes connecting with recruiters, employers and personal and professional contacts; and solid preparation for your job interviews. Mastering these elements should greatly enhance your job prospects.

THE RESUME

This crucial calling card needs to be a standout. Above all, it should highlight what you have *achieved*, not what you have *done*. And it needs to be specific. Examples of achievements could include your ideas that boosted sales by, say, 50 percent, three new products your team launched or the number of clients you brought to the firm.

Keep the resume to two pages. But make sure it includes your education, training or classes that have improved your skills, and outside interests and memberships relevant to the job you're seeking.

And be careful about semantics. Since many recruiters and companies use automated screening to help comb through a pile of resumes, wording can help or hinder your ability to get noticed. To turn the system to your advantage, include certain terms, such as an accounting practice or medical equipment you use, which convey your experience. But avoid words that signal age, such as the name of a long-defunct employer or skills no longer in use. Also avoid listing jobs held in the distant past.

Any gaps in the resume? Don't skirt the issue. Employers are aware that many older women have experienced periods away from the workforce. Reasons could include joblessness, illness, time out for education or training or a hiatus to deal with divorce or widowhood or caring for family members. While resumes typically wouldn't mention personal/family issues, an interviewer likely will inquire about them. Prepare to discuss these job forays: the ways they furthered your personal growth and how you kept abreast of your profession while away from the workplace.

Being forthright is important. According to a study by Vanderbilt law and economics professors Joni Hersch and Jennifer Bennett Shinall, a female job applicant raises her chances of getting hired if she provides personal information clarifying gaps in her work history during job interviews. Evidently, the reverse is also true: the study found that "concealing personal information lowers female applicants' job prospects." Why? The report cited "the behavioral economics theory of ambiguity aversion," which holds that "individuals prefer known risks over unknown risks," stated the Vanderbilt law professors.[3]

NETWORKING

Once your resume is complete, you'll need job prospects, which networking can help provide. Cast your net widely. Beyond family and friends, extend your outreach to social networking sites, school alumni associations and organizations where you're a member, and sign up to participate at events sponsored by trade and professional associations. Let people know you are job hunting and would value their assistance.

Be strategic in your use of social media. Steer clear of discussing politics, work gripes or deeply personal information; such topics can raise red flags with potential employers. Instead, post material that enhances your professional stature. And sign up for—or expand your use of—LinkedIn. "This powerful social media site is geared to professionals," says Lindsey McMillion Stemann, of McMillion Consulting, which specializes in the use of LinkedIn. On that platform you can highlight your skills and achievements, build a wide network of contacts, post commentary that gets you noticed and apply for listed jobs. Indeed, more than 90 percent of recruiters use LinkedIn to search for job candidates, Lindsey reports.

In addition, you could explore some job search internet sites that cater to older workers. Among these are Workforce50.com, Retirement Jobs.com and jobs.aarp.org.

TAPPING CONTACTS

Maintaining professional and personal contacts is always advisable. When you're job hunting, these people could be essential to your success. And you never know who might come through for you, or when. Consider the experiences of Vineeta Anand, Susan Avery and Diane Bruno.

Vineeta Anand, a divorcée living in Alexandria, Virginia, got her current job at age 60 thanks to an executive she had interviewed for an article when she was a reporter, 15 years earlier. She had left journalism and had spent her 50s as an analyst at a major international union in Washington, DC; 10 years later, facing early retirement, she tapped her network—including the executive she'd once interviewed—to find another job.

She had kept in touch with the executive over the years. As she began looking for work, she used LinkedIn to reconnect with him and then emailed to invite him for coffee or lunch whenever he would be in Washington.

Six months later, he asked her to lunch. When she learned, by asking, that his business—an actuarial firm he had started—did not have a public-relations official, she took the initiative: she suggested he contact her if they decided to hire one. A month later, Vineeta was called in for an interview and subsequently landed the job.

Susan Avery has seen how doing good deeds can be rewarding—in an unexpected way.

Her story began years ago, when she, a former journalist and editor, helped her niece and nephew with their college applications. From there, she began assisting her friends' children with their applications. "I would be helping 10 children at any given time," recalls Susan, who was "doing it free-of-charge because I enjoyed helping kids."

But at age 54, the New Yorker was job hunting after the company where she'd been working—a news start-up—folded. Although interviews for new jobs went well, offers didn't follow. Her executive recruiter attributed it to ageism.

Eventually, however, Susan was contacted by the principal of a two-year-old high school who was seeking a counselor to help students applying to college. She had learned about Susan from the mother of a child Susan had once helped.

The recommendation opened the door to a whole new career: Susan started as a college counselor, working three days a week. But after several years and a teaching fellowship program, Susan became a full-fledged high school teacher.

For Diane Bruno, of Connecticut, it paid off to contact a recruiter personally—not just submit a resume. Using LinkedIn, she once reached out and introduced herself to the executive hiring for a job she wanted. After seven interviews, Diane landed the job.

Over the years, Diane has successfully changed careers, switching from communications to funeral directing and back to communications. When seeking a job after leaving the funeral business, she found some interviewers intrigued by her stint as a funeral director. "Some found it fascinating and somewhat empowering," she recalls. "They felt that, if I could handle a family at the worst time in their lives"— when a loved one had died—"I could handle anything."

THE INTERVIEW

Once your resume or contacts have gotten you an interview, there are still more minefields to clear. Ageism, and especially appearance-based ageism, are still problems and a quiet form of discrimination. Overcome these hurdles by presenting yourself confidently, and be ready to field even tough interview questions.

Appearance

Every woman has a story of someone who tried to go gracefully gray but then returned to hair coloring to stay employed. Your hair color—if it's gray—could matter in the United States' youth-centric culture. But happily, its impact on your job hunt shrinks or disappears if your reputation precedes you or if the job you want welcomes older workers.

As a standard option, consider wearing a dress to an interview. However, depending on the profession or industry, experts say options can include anything from smart business casual, if interviewing with a tech company, to a pantsuit with a finance or law firm to an outfit with flair if you're heading to a fashion house. For clues as to the appropriate garb, check the company's social media sites for photos of employees attending company events.

Acing the Interview

Do your homework before you go, and learn about the company. Bone up on the organization, combing through its website, reading articles about the firm and perusing its annual report. Check social media sites to glean what people are posting about the organization. And speak to friends who now, or previously, worked there. In addition, learn what you can about the person who will interview you; any common ground that you can slip into the conversation, such as schools you both attended, can make you more memorable.

And think creatively about how you can stand out. During her interview, Vineeta Anand gave a PowerPoint presentation showing what she could do for the actuarial firm that eventually hired her.

Before the interview, prepare answers to likely questions along with issues and points you'd like to make. For instance, ask why this position is available now, and after you receive a response, explain why, under those circumstances, you're perfect for the job. Also, be ready to assess the organization's products and services, if asked, and anticipate questions such as "Why do you want to work here?" and "How would you handle . . . ?" a particular problem or situation. To deflect possible—unspoken—concerns about your age, bring up situations that reflected your energy and creativity.

It's all in how you present yourself. Although you can't make yourself younger, you can demonstrate how well you adapt to any situation. Above all, project self-confidence, and don't seem overanxious. "No matter how much you need or want that job, you cannot appear desperate," cautions Vineeta Anand. "Say to yourself, 'I am very good and I deserve this job. But if I don't get it, it's their loss, and I will find a better job.'"

If you get a job offer, you may have to be flexible. Depending on the job market, you may be offered a lower-than-desired salary, especially if you're changing careers. If you can't get the pay you need in a new profession, consider remaining in your current one. The choices can be tough. Salary can be a real factor for single women, says CoveyClub's Lesley Jane Seymour, especially for those who are also supporting parents or children. But you have the advantage of experience with office politics and negotiations: "You know the tricks already, so you're likely to move up fast," says Lesley. Keep the door open so you can negotiate for more money later.

And don't ignore job benefits—offerings that could include health and other insurance, a retirement savings plan, paid sick days, a family leave policy and more. These benefits can be vital to your career and pocketbook, especially if you're not old enough for Medicare and/or have children at home.

For Susan Avery, getting health insurance was a key attraction to her current job. As a single mother by choice—with no other parent to help—she's needed the coverage, both for herself and her 20-something daughter. Working mainly as a freelancer in theater production, her daughter has lacked access to employer-sponsored insurance. By obtaining insurance through her employer, Susan saves almost $20,000 a year over what she'd have to pay out of pocket for coverage.

GOING FULL CIRCLE

To be sure, job hunting, even after age 55, can take you down unexpected paths—or back to the trail you were once following and may have thought you'd left behind. Consider the odyssey of Shannon Michael, of Salt Lake City, who moved to New York in her late 50s, leaving behind a spouse and adult children. She had been recruited to work with a national public relations firm in New York. But the job proved to be a poor fit, and after almost three years, she decided to return west. "My husband and I had some marriage repair to do," she says.

Back in Utah, Shannon soon found work leading communications at an education technology company. But she was facing another mismatch. "The worksite was a classic technology office, with hoverboards and Ping-Pong tables, kitchens everywhere and horrible food," she remembers. And the office environment had a fair amount of "age snobbery—a sense that you couldn't be cool if you were over age 40." Things worsened for her after Shannon shared with a manager that she had been undergoing treatments for uterine cancer when she'd started—getting chemotherapy in mornings before work. (She is now cancer-free.) A week after divulging this news, she was called into a manager's office and told she was not a good fit for the team. But she received a generous severance because she'd recorded the manager labeling her situation "a generational thing."

The severance helped when her son—who had been working on a cruise ship in Asia—was diagnosed with a brain tumor (from which he recovered). But in the five weeks she watched over her adult son in the hospital, Shannon realized what she wanted to do next: "Work with grown-ups," she said, "and not with the skateboard kids."

Shannon reached out to someone she had known, the owner of a small public relations firm in the Salt Lake City area who hired only senior-level employees. Initially, she joined the staff, but once she qualified for Medicare, she chose to become an outside contractor. Professionally, Shannon had come full circle. She was back in public relations, but this time on her own terms.

6

DEBT—AND HOW TO
GET OUT OF IT

Debt is a small word with potentially huge consequences. It can sneak up on you. You may have a medical emergency or car repairs you can't pay for out of pocket. Or, like Jenna, a 30-something single woman in Ohio, you can wisely invest in education and home ownership—only to be left with a mountain of debt.

However helpful borrowing may be—providing funds for an immediate purchase or an education—it comes with a price. If you don't repay your loan right away, interest on it accrues, driving up the overall price of what you bought. The higher the interest on your loan, the harder the escape from debt. Digging out can feel as futile as shoveling snow during a blizzard.

But you can escape the debt trap. With planning, you can make smart, necessary, even big-ticket purchases using debt. The trick is to plan an exit strategy—a way to pay off loans as soon as possible and with a clear finish line. As Jenna found, you need ways to control debt so that it doesn't affect your finances and quality of life.

Jenna recently completed a master's degree in clinical mental health counseling and faces $150,000 of student debt in addition to her mortgage. But Jenna has a plan to make her investments, in a home and in education, work in her favor despite their high cost. Her house purchase already provides her with valuable home equity. And Jenna is working hard to pay off her student loans. In addition to her full-time job at a nearby prison, she has a part-time job resulting from a paid internship she had while in school. Oh, and there's the government angle she's working: to help scale her mountain of student debt, Jenna plans to use the federal Public Service Loan Forgiveness Program; it provides some student loan relief for borrowers who work in designated sectors, such as the local prison system.

So a way out is available, even if you're feeling swamped by your debt—from student loans to unpaid credit card balances, mortgages and more. It takes knowing where to find help. And knowing whom to avoid, especially payday lenders.

CREDIT CARD DEBT

Credit cards have distinctive pros and cons. On the bright side, they provide a convenient payment method, and their monthly statements can help you track expenses. But if you don't pay off your account balances every month, the cards quickly become a burden. You'll owe interest, often 18 percent or higher, on the unpaid balance. And paying the minimum amount each month hardly makes a dent. In fact, if you pay $50 a month on a $5,000 credit card balance, you'll need more than 30 years to pay it off. Your monthly payments will add up to $40,000 over those 30 years.

Since women typically earn less than men, many women find it harder to afford debt repayments, data show. Consider the results of a study commissioned by CompareCards.com: only 33 percent of women surveyed said they had paid off their full credit card balance within the past year, compared to 40 percent of men.[1] According to a study by Federal Reserve Board staff, single women under age 40 who earned less than $200,000 had lower credit scores, more debt and more past-due payments reported on their credit histories than did single males of that age and income.[2]

There is a way out of credit card debt. It starts by examining your expenditures, seeing what you can cut or reduce to free up funds for debt repayment and then mapping how you'll pay off what you owe.

If you typically pay by credit card, as many people do, use your card's history of your spending activity to help guide you in the right spending direction.

Here's a way it can work: gather the last six months of credit card and bank statements and sort the charges into spending categories such as groceries, clothing, entertainment, personal care and vacations, among other groups. From there, compare monthly balances to determine what, if any, spending you can cut. Next, create a spending plan—a budget that includes all your expenses, including those that occur quarterly or every six months, such as property taxes and car insurance. Then compare your spending plan with your actual outlays in each category over the past month. To get help on the internet, look for the worksheets in the Savings Fitness booklet, available from the Department of Labor, at www.dol.gov, or the tracking systems of Mint, at www.mint.com, and YNAB (You Need a Budget), at www .YNAB.com.

Once you have examined your spending, plan how to pay the credit card debt. Two recommended approaches are the "snowball" and "roll-down" methods.

Here's how they work: set aside a sum, say, $300, for monthly credit card payments. First, pay the minimum balances on your cards. Then, with funds remaining from the $300 (let's say it's $100), you make a choice: you can use the $100 to pay off a larger chunk of the balance on the card with the smallest balance (the snowball technique), or you can make a larger payment on the balance of the card with the highest interest rate (the roll-down method). Once you've paid off one card's balance, move on to the next one. Make larger payments on the card with the next smallest balance, if you're using the snowball method, or the card with the next-highest interest rate, if using the roll-down technique. If you stick to the plan, eventually you will erase all your credit card debt.

You can compare the results of using the snowball method versus the roll-down method using calculators on the website www.dinky town.net. You will likely spend less on interest charges using the roll-down approach, but you may prefer eliminating the number of cards with balances more quickly using the snowball technique.

If you lack the funds to make a larger-than-minimum monthly payment, it may be necessary to cut some discretionary spending. Potential candidates could include cable TV, restaurant dining or other nonessentials. But don't discard items that are important to you and can motivate you to stay on track.

If funds become extremely tight, contact your credit card company rather than forgoing payments. As the Consumer Financial Protection Bureau recommends, ask credit card companies to postpone a few payments, lower the interest rate or allow you to pay a smaller monthly amount.[3] If you don't get relief from the card operators, consider consulting a nonprofit credit counselor about creating a debt management plan (DMP). Your counselor will negotiate an affordable repayment plan—typically over three to five years—with your credit card companies. You'll make one monthly payment to the credit counselor, who then pays your creditors. This service may require a start-up cost as well as a small monthly fee. Find nonprofit credit counselors at www.NFCC.org.

But avoid so-called debt relief companies. As the Consumer Financial Protection Bureau warns, these firms charge high and often hidden fees and may land you deeper in debt.[4]

For recent widows or divorcées, there's good and bad news. The positive news for recent widows: although rules vary by state, you generally aren't responsible for your late spouse's credit card debt if you were not a joint holder on the card account, points out Karen Chan, an independent personal finance educator. The bad news for recent divorcées: if you are still a holder of the card account, don't assume you can avoid paying the balance on the account just because the divorce decree says so. If you are still listed as a holder of the account, you are likely liable for the debt if your ex doesn't pay.

MEDICAL DEBT

It's not surprising that as many as 40 percent of personal bankruptcies can be traced to hospital and doctor bills. And you may be vulnerable to a financial crisis caused by medical debt even if you are young and insured.

Barbi was 37 when she was diagnosed with breast cancer. She did not work for weeks while receiving treatment and, although she qualified under the Family and Medical Leave Act (FMLA) to continue her insurance and other benefits, her paychecks stopped. For years, Barbi had worked hard to keep her debt manageable. She researched and won scholarships at a local university and signed up for a low-cost mortgage through the USDA Rural Development program. But when her monthly income dried up, she maxed out her credit cards to stay afloat. And then the medical bills started to pile up. Barbi had health insurance through her employer, but many of her expenses were not covered. Now, after months of treatment and four surgeries, she owes over $15,000 in medical debt. She is trying to arrange manageable monthly payments, but it is a long and frustrating process when various hospitals and doctors are involved.

Women should not let hospitals and doctors pressure them into paying medical bills ahead of other obligations, holds Karen Chan. If other bills require more immediate attention—such as an urgent car repair that needs on-the-spot payment—take care of that bill first. If you can't immediately pay off a medical or hospital bill, Chan recommends asking the hospital's or doctor's billing office for a payment arrangement. Offer an affordable monthly amount and ask if interest charges can be waived. While it may take more than one attempt, medical providers often accommodate such requests for help.

If you can't reach an agreement, medical claims advocates could negotiate a lower payment on your behalf. You will likely pay them an hourly rate plus a percentage of the money you save. Search for advocates on the website of the Alliance of Claims Assistance Professionals (www.claims.org).

MORTGAGES

Your home is likely your largest purchase and, if you own one, your mortgage is probably your largest debt. But however burdensome, a mortgage does offer some attractions:

- The loan gives you the opportunity to buy a home, which provides shelter and an important financial asset. Some data show that, for many single women, homeownership accounts for a substantial part of net worth.
- You can pocket all the profits when you sell. When you buy a house with a mortgage, you share ownership with the bank. When you sell the house, however, your lender gets only the loan balance. You keep the difference between the sales price and the mortgage, including any price appreciation.
- The monthly payment on a fixed-rate mortgage doesn't increase, even though inflation boosts the cost of most goods and services.
- By refinancing, you can change the terms of your mortgage. If interest rates decline after you purchase your home, you often can switch to a lower rate and either lower your monthly payment or reduce the years left on your mortgage. But what if interest rates rise? Sit back and smile: you're locked into an attractive low rate.
- Purchasing a home with a mortgage ties up less of your money in home ownership, freeing up more funds to invest. Mortgage interest rates are typically lower than the average return on a mix of stocks and bonds. Thus you earn more by investing rather than paying off your mortgage ahead of time. For example, say a single woman—we'll call her Jan—pays an additional $1,200 a year toward her 30-year fixed mortgage, starting in year five. After Jan pays off her mortgage—about five and a half years earlier than scheduled—she invests what had been her monthly mortgage payment, plus the extra $1,200 per year, in a diversified mutual fund. However, Jan hadn't considered that investments typically return more than the interest you pay on mortgages. Thus she ended up with almost 40 percent less in her investment account than her cousin Fran, who chose to invest earlier rather than paying extra on her mortgage. After 30 years, both women have paid off their mortgage but, as figure 6.1 on the next page shows, Fran has accumulated more savings.
- Last and, for most single women, least, is the mortgage tax break. Generally, mortgage interest is tax deductible, but in order to capture that benefit, you must itemize. In 2017, Congress almost

doubled the standard deduction, and now only one in six taxpayers itemizes. For most people, the standard deduction is the better option, and that means no tax benefit for having a mortgage.

As useful as mortgages are, not every loan is suitable for your situation. To avoid problems down the road, follow these guidelines:

- Shop around. Get quotes from two or three lenders and compare the APR (Annual Percentage Rate), which includes the interest rate and all fees and points.
- Don't take a mortgage that exceeds your needs. Since mortgage payments can account for a huge chunk of your income, keep your home loan to the minimum you need.
- Think carefully about which type of mortgage you want—a fixed-rate or an adjustable-rate mortgage (ARM). An ARM can be enticing because the interest rate is initially lower than that on most fixed-rate mortgages, but a rise in interest rates will boost the cost of your mortgage payment. In contrast, you lock in your rate and avoid surprises with a fixed-rate mortgage.

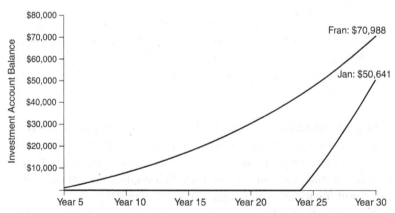

Note: Jan pays $1,200 more toward her mortgage each year beginning in Year 5. After paying off her mortgage (in mid-Year 24), Jan invests the mortgage payment plus $1,200 per year in a mutual fund. Fran pays her regular mortgage payment and invests $1,200 per year in a mutual fund beginning in Year 5.

Figure 6.1. Paying Off Mortgage Early (Jan) vs. Investing (Fran). *Source:* Authors.

What if you already have a 30-year fixed mortgage and now interest rates are lower than when you obtained the loan? Should you refinance? The answer depends on the cost to refinance compared with the amount you could save on your monthly payments, as well as the time you expect to keep your current home. An example: if you will save $100 a month by refinancing and the closing costs come to $2,400, you will break even in two years. In this example, as long as you plan to stay in your home more than two years, it will pay to refinance.

STUDENT LOANS

Student loan balances are soaring—doubling in the past 10 years—and, as of this writing, exceed total credit card debt in the United States. Even as demands for reform of the system—including loan forgiveness and tuition-free community college—have intensified, loan default rates have spiraled, especially among students in for-profit colleges. According to the Brookings Institution, 43 percent of students who enrolled in a for-profit college in 2004 defaulted on their loans within 12 years, compared to 23 percent of those who enrolled in 1996.[5]

Since the amount you can borrow from the government is capped, many students get a mix of public and private loans. To manage private student loans, be sure to repay them promptly. And if possible, negotiate a lower interest rate or several months of interest-only payments.

If you have public (also called federal) student loans, you have an array of repayment options. Start by getting a statement of your loans at https://studentaid.gov. You may be able to consolidate your federal loans (through the same website) and stretch out your repayment term from the standard 10 years to as long as 30 years, depending on how much you owe. You will end up with a single, lower monthly payment, but it will take you longer to pay off your debt.

Alternatively, if refinancing, you may get a lower rate on your federal debt with a private lender, such as a bank. But be careful: if you use a private loan to repay your public student debt, you will lose the repayment options available only on federal loans, such as basing your monthly payment on a percentage of your discretionary income.

As of this writing, five repayment plans are available: Income-Contingent Repayment (ICR), Income-Based Repayment (IBR), Pay as You Earn (PAYE), Revised Pay as You Earn (REPAYE) and Income-Sensitive Repayment (ISR). After making payments for 10 to 25 years, depending on the plan, any remaining loan balance vanishes. Previously, loan forgiveness often came with a sting because you paid taxes on the forgiven balance. The American Rescue Plan corrects that by making tax-free all student loans forgiven or cancelled between January 1, 2021, and December 31, 2025.

The choice of plan varies with your personal and financial situation. An especially attractive option is the Public Service Loan Forgiveness (PSLF) program—the strategy Jenna chose. To qualify, you must work for the federal, state or local government or for a nonprofit organization, and you must make 120 income-based payments on your federal direct student loans. Although payments do not have to be consecutive, you must keep meticulous records and document your employment every year. If you follow the rules, any remaining federal debt is forgiven tax-free in as few as 10 years.

To compare your options, enter your information in the Loan Simulator tool on the www.studentaid.gov website. Let's say you owe $75,000 in unsubsidized federal student loans with a current interest rate of 4.5 percent, you earn $50,000 a year, and you expect to receive a 2 percent annual raise. Your options for paying off your debt range from plans with no loan forgiveness to the Public Service option that effectively forgives two-thirds of your loan (including interest), as shown in table 6.1.

Table 6.1. Three Options for Repaying a Federal Student Loan

Federal Student Loan Repayment Plan	Monthly Payment	Number of Years Paid	Total Amount Paid	Amount Forgiven
Standard Plan	$777	10	$93,240	$0
Extended Fixed Plan	$418	25	$125,062	$0
Income-Based Plan with Public Service Loan Forgiveness	Between $242 and $248	10	$31,355	$77,395

Source: Loan Simulator on the Federal Student Aid website.
Note: Assumes a $75,000 federal loan at 4.5 percent interest and holder of loan earns $50,000 per year, is single and expects a 2 percent annual raise.

You may also be eligible for the Public Service Loan Forgiveness program if you took out PLUS loans (Parent Loan for Undergraduate Students) to pay for your child's education and you work for the government or a nonprofit organization.

If you are considering graduate study or finishing up your undergraduate work, minimize the amount you borrow. Of course, you'll want to explore financial aid for single women or single moms from your university. And if employed, check your benefits: some employers provide up to $5,250 tax-free for tuition and other expenses. If unemployed, consider lining up a paid internship, as Jenna did, to help with expenses.

GUARDING YOUR CREDIT

Your credit score can make or break your financial life. A low score can prevent you from getting an attractive rate on a mortgage or car loan—or from qualifying for any loan. You may have trouble renting an apartment or landing a job—particularly in the financial services industry—if your score is below average. And your home and auto insurance premiums may increase if your score drops.

Be sure to review your credit at least annually. Start by seeking your credit report from each of the three main credit bureaus—Equifax, TransUnion and Experian—all available at www.annualcreditreport. com (or by calling 877-322-8228). If there's a mistake, contact the credit bureau directly using the Federal Trade Commission's sample letter found on its website, www.FTC.gov. The credit bureau must respond to you within 30 days.

PAYDAY LOANS

Don't go there. These schemes—marketed as funds for an emergency—charge exorbitant interest rates and will drown you in debt.

If you need a small loan to cover an emergency, check for any assistance or benefits your employer may provide, or apply for a loan from your local credit union or bank. (Smaller banks may be more accommodating.) Even adding to your credit card balance is preferable to paying 400 percent interest on a payday loan. If you own a home, you may able to arrange a home equity line of credit (HELOC). The best way to cover unexpected costs is to create an emergency fund. Having savings for a rainy day means you don't have to scramble if an emergency occurs. Being prepared is a ticket to financial peace of mind.

7

INVESTING SMART

Tech stocks are overvalued. The market's rotation favors cyclicals. A wave of program trading hit the market . . . credit default swaps. . . .

When you see or hear such Wall Street gobbledygook, your eyes may glaze over. Or you may simply tune out. Understandably, this jargon doesn't strike a chord. It may even sound intimidating.

But don't be put off. The kind of straightforward, sensible investing you can and should do isn't wrapped in a foreign-sounding language. It's not geared to PhDs. It's a logical process of making your savings grow to meet your needs and goals, using traditional vehicles such as stocks, bonds, cash and maybe real estate. You allocate your savings among these options (and possibly others, if you're an experienced investor willing to take extra risk) and then periodically review your holdings for any needed adjustments. Because you're investing for the long term, you avoid missteps: you don't "time the market" for presumed "hot" buys or dump stocks if the market suddenly swoons.

Happily, you can map your own investment strategy. Or you can seek guidance from a professional. Either way, you'll find investing to be a vital and fruitful method of securing your financial future.

To be sure, the topic of investing is littered with misperceptions. Some of the distracting myths to ignore include:

Myth #1: *You need to be a math whiz to understand investing.* No. The process is straightforward and easy to grasp when explained.

Myth #2: *Professional investors have the inside scoop, so they can beat the market.* Untrue. No one—not even Warren Buffett—has consistently, year after year, racked up returns higher than a market index such as the S&P 500. After all, who predicted the coronavirus in 2020 would ravage the economy and distort the markets? The best formula is to invest steadily and stay the course.

Myth #3: *Investing is a man's game.* Au contraire. Women are often the better investors. In a study by Barber and Odean, the data showed women earned almost 1 percent more on their investments than did men, on average. Single women fared even better, beating single men by more than 1.4 percent.[1] That 1.4 percent annual difference snowballs into a 30 percent advantage over 20 years. The authors concluded that men tend to be overconfident, which leads them to buy and sell investments more frequently than women, swelling their trading costs and lowering their returns.

Haleh Moddasser, financial advisor and author of *Women on Top: Women, Wealth and Social Change*, finds that women are often better investors than men because they take a long view on their investing and avoid swinging in and out of the market. "Once women are in, they stay the course," says Haleh, "and that serves them well over the long run."

Myth #4: *You can eliminate risk by sticking to safe investments such as Certificates of Deposit (CDs) and bank accounts.* No. You simply won't earn enough on CDs or your bank account to grow the retirement savings you'll eventually need. In fact, inflation can swamp the small returns you do get from such low-yielding investments, leaving you back where you started in terms of purchasing power. In exchange for the stability of bank accounts, you take on another risk: the danger your money won't grow enough to last your lifetime. If you're looking to boost savings over time, invest a portion of your money in stocks.

THE BASICS

So where to start? The first steps include defining your goals and figuring out how soon you will need the money. If you are saving for the down payment on a home in five years, put the money in low-risk investments such as bond mutual funds, I Bonds (savings bonds that adjust with inflation) and CDs. Since you need the money soon, avoid stocks with their unpredictable short-term returns. When do stocks come into play? When you're investing for longer-term goals, such as retirement and children's education. In fact, the longer your time horizon, the more you can—and should—invest in stocks. Say you aim to retire in 12 years. If you had invested $1,000 a year in a S&P 500 fund beginning in 2005, you would have accumulated $23,000 by your retirement date—90 percent more than the $12,000 you put in. And by investing over a long period, you were able to "ride out" the market's peaks and troughs—including the 2008 market crash. However, over the same 12-year period, if you had kept your money in CDs earning 3 percent annually, your account would only have reached roughly $14,000—40 percent less than if you had invested in stocks.

These examples were based on a particular historical period, but the message is clear: load up on fixed investments such as CDs and bonds for money you'll need in five years or less, but for longer term goals, put at least half of your savings in stocks. Although you may trim your stock holdings as you approach retirement, don't eliminate them. You will need to earn more than CD rates to sustain a retirement that could last 20 to 30 years.

TYPES OF INVESTMENTS

To reduce the chance your investments will be whipsawed by rapid swings in the market, spread out your holdings among stocks, bonds, cash and, perhaps, real estate. You may hear about "alternative investments," such as commodities and hedge funds, but these options are very risky and expensive to buy and sell, and, overall, they should be avoided.

How do you choose investments? The first step is to understand the role each type of investment—or asset—plays. Stocks, also called equities, represent ownership in a company. When you purchase stock in a company, you effectively become one of its owners. You can make money two ways: when the price of your shares grows higher than the price you paid for it and when the company pays a dividend to shareholders. Newer, smaller companies, and even a few big companies (like Warren Buffett's Berkshire Hathaway), do not pay dividends, so you only make money if the price of your shares appreciates.

Bonds work differently. Organizations, such as the US government or corporations, issue bonds when they wish to borrow money to finance spending or pay off other debt. When you buy a bond, you lend money to the organization. In return, you receive a promise to be repaid in full when the bond matures, along with interest, which is typically paid every six months.

You can invest in individual bonds or, better yet, mutual funds. These funds are "baskets" of securities; when you buy shares in a bond fund, you effectively invest in a very small slice of hundreds or thousands of different bonds. The funds are professionally managed, saving you the trouble of researching and tracking individual bonds. Shares of bond funds do not "mature" as individual bonds do; instead, the price of the shares is determined by market conditions. That means the value of your account can fluctuate.

Bonds and interest rates move in opposite directions; typically, the price of bonds rise when interest rates decline. While bonds are rarely dazzling performers, they are less volatile than stocks and can be a safer haven in times when the stock market languishes.

Of the various types of bonds, Treasury securities are the safest because they are issued and backed by the US government. Treasuries include bills, which mature in one year or less; notes, which come due between 2 and 10 years after purchase and pay interest twice a year; and bonds, which mature beyond 10 years and also pay interest semiannually. The federal government also issues Treasury Inflation-Protected Securities (TIPS), which pay interest twice a year and whose value increases with the rate of inflation. You can purchase Treasury bills, notes, bonds, TIPS and savings bonds directly from the government at TreasuryDirect, www.treasurydirect.gov, or through a brokerage firm.

US savings bonds are a popular way to loan money to the government. You can purchase up to a total of $10,000 of EE savings bonds or I savings bonds annually. I bonds pay a fixed rate of interest plus an inflation "bonus," which typically adds up to a higher rate than that paid on EE bonds or most bank accounts. Savings bonds are familiar investments and, like Treasuries, are extremely safe. Both EE and I savings bonds mature in 30 years and, along the way, continue to accrue interest. But you must hold them for at least 12 months before selling and, if you cash them in within 5 years of purchase, you lose 3 months' worth of interest.

You don't pay income tax on the interest earned on savings bonds until you sell them—and then you only pay federal tax. Savings bond interest is exempt from state and local taxes. You may be able to cash in savings bonds completely tax-free if the money is used to pay qualified college expenses for you or your children.

State and local governments also issue bonds, called municipal bonds, or "munis." Interest from these debt issues, which help fund infrastructure projects for a state, city or county, is free of federal income tax. It may also be free of state taxes if you buy the bonds issued by your state or city. These are attractive investments for those looking to cut their tax bill, and they typically offer a higher interest rate than the safer Treasury bonds.

The third type of asset is cash. Besides the money in your wallet, this includes checking, savings and money market accounts as well as CDs. Cash is a low-risk, low-return investment, best used for stashing money you will need within the next year or two.

A fourth investment category to consider is real estate. Different from stocks and bonds, this brick-and-mortar holding is not usually something you trade (forget house flipping). Typically, it's the huge outlay you make for a basic need: shelter. Less commonly, it may be a property you own and rent for income. Although this investment may appreciate over time and has tax advantages, it also comes with ongoing expenses, such as a mortgage, property taxes and repairs. Given the costs involved, you'll need to think carefully about this big commitment, lest the expenses overwhelm your budget. If you don't want to own a home, you can invest in property through real estate investment trusts (REITs). Like mutual funds, these trusts own a variety of holdings such as shopping centers, office buildings and other commercial real estate.

Bear in mind that these asset classes do not move in lockstep, and it's impossible to predict their next move. In 2008, stocks lost over 36 percent of their value, but US Treasury bonds sparkled, earning 20 percent. If you had shifted your investments in the hope of a repeat performance, you would have been deeply disappointed. The next year, fortunes reversed and stocks rose almost 26 percent, while Treasury bonds lost 11 percent.[2]

Generally, the higher the average return, the higher the risk. Stocks tend to chalk up enviable returns over time, as shown in figure 7.1, but a portfolio invested exclusively in stocks is just too unpredictable.

Similarly, the lowest-risk investments—Treasuries—tend to score the lowest returns over time. Yet they provide a cushion when stocks are plummeting. That's why it's important to diversify your investments. When stocks are riding high, the returns from bonds and cash look pretty measly. But the 5 percent average return earned by corporate bonds is welcome when stocks are in the red.

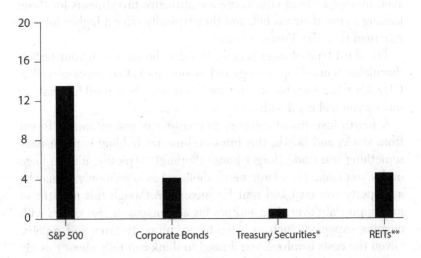

Returns are total returns, including reinvestment of dividends and capital gains.
* 1-5 year Treasury Securities
**Real Estate Investment Trusts

Figure 7.1. Average Annual Return of Stocks, Bonds and REITs: 10-Year Period Ending December 31, 2020. *Source*: Morningstar, Inc.

ALLOCATING YOUR INVESTMENTS

How do you spread out your investments among the different asset classes? First, figure out roughly when you'll need the money—whether it's near term or later on—and then determine how much investment risk your nerves can handle.

As mentioned earlier, the sooner you'll need the money, the more you should invest in short-term, low-risk holdings such as CDs or money market funds. If you'll need the savings in anywhere between one and five years, create a safe but slightly better-returning mix of bonds and some cash. And beyond five years, pepper up your portfolio with stocks. As a general rule of thumb, the longer your time horizon, the more money you can invest in stocks.

But that rule of thumb also depends on your risk tolerance—your ability to withstand market surges and dives without bailing out. How do you gauge your risk tolerance? One helpful tool could be the risk assessment tool available on the Charles Schwab website, www.schwab.com (search for Investor Profile Questionnaire). After answering a few questions, you can get a risk tolerance score and view sample portfolio allocations that match your risk profile. As an example, figure 7.2 (below) shows the suggested allotment for a moderate investor.

After you select an allocation, live with it for several months to ensure that you're comfortable with it. If you lose sleep every time stocks have a bad day, sell some of them and reinvest the money in cash or bonds. Or if you are investing in a 401(k) plan or IRA, for example, switch your contributions to a bond fund until you reach a comfortable allocation. Then stick to this formula rather than reacting to or trying to anticipate market swings.

About once a year, check your allocation. If the portion of investments in any asset class is more than 5 percent higher or lower than your intended allocation, make adjustments. Let's say your target is 35 percent devoted to large-company stocks but those investments have benefited from a rising market and are now worth 40 percent of your portfolio. Sell shares of stock funds and invest the proceeds in bond funds or cash until the allocations line up with your intended split. By rebalancing, you avoid holding too many eggs in a basket—which can make your portfolio riskier than you had intended.

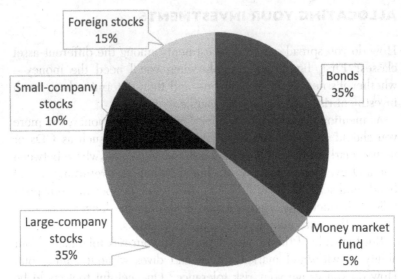

Figure 7.2. Suggested Investment Allocation for a Moderate-Risk Portfolio. *Source:* Schwab Investor Profile Questionnaire at https://www.schwab.com /public/file/P-778947.

CHOOSING INVESTMENTS

Once you've decided to split up your investments among different asset classes, the next step is selecting the investments within the classes you've chosen. For the majority of individual investors, choosing individual stocks and bonds is simply too time consuming and difficult. To diversify your holdings adequately, you would need to invest in at least 30 stocks and 30 bonds, according to many experts. Most of us are not trained to wade through the pages of reports and analysis to ferret out promising stocks. Besides, trying to choose stocks that outperform the rest of the market is, ultimately, a fruitless endeavor.

Instead, you can assemble a diversified, low-cost portfolio by investing in mutual funds or exchange-traded funds (ETFs). By purchasing shares in a fund, you turn over the responsibility of selecting investments to the fund manager. But how do you choose among the thousands of funds?

If you are investing in a 401(k) or similar plan at work, your task is easier: you get a set menu of investment choices. At a minimum, you can expect a stock, bond and cash option and often choices such as a large-capitalization (large-cap) stock fund (which invests in large companies), a small-cap fund and an international stock fund. Many 401(k) plans also offer target-date funds, "one-stop-shopping" funds that tailor investments to the date you expect to retire and then automatically adjust the allocation each year. Their mix starts with a heavy weighting in stocks for young investors but gradually becomes tamer—more conservatively invested—as you approach retirement.

Investing in a 401(k) plan has other attractions. Typically, the money you invest is automatically deducted from your paycheck. This process, called "dollar-cost-averaging," keeps you from reacting to major market swings. And by investing the same amount each month, you buy more shares at a lower price when the market declines.

But what if you need to pick funds yourself, say, for your Individual Retirement Account (IRA)? Suddenly, your choices explode. And within the universe of funds, your options range widely from the type of investment—mutual funds or ETFs—to management style to asset class.

Mutual funds invest in a variety of securities, often in a particular category, such as large-cap stocks or Treasury bonds. The funds can be actively managed, meaning securities are individually selected by the fund manager, or passively managed, meaning the funds replicate and generally perform in line with a specific index, such as the S&P 500 index. Active managers try to beat their target index but often fall short of even matching their benchmark. According to Morningstar, a company that compiles investment data, only 24 percent of actively managed funds were able to hit or beat their target over the 10-year period ending June 2020.[3] And fees charged by active managers typically exceed those charged by passively managed funds. In the long run, individual investors likely do better by sticking to passively managed funds, among them, "index" funds.

Another option is ETFs—collections of securities that typically replicate a market index. These funds, now numbering almost 7,000, are bought and sold on an exchange, similar to how stocks are traded. Like index mutual funds, ETFs have lower expenses than actively managed funds.

So how do you whittle down the list of mutual funds and ETFs? First, you want to rule out all the mutual funds that charge extra fees, such as loads or commissions. You pay an up-front charge of about 5 percent of your investment or as much as an extra 1 percent per year when you buy a load fund from a broker or advisor who sells products. These costs are in addition to regular, ongoing expenses and are deducted before the fund's earnings are calculated. It's not surprising that load funds consistently underperform the no-load variety you buy directly from a mutual fund company such as Vanguard or T. Rowe Price. To determine how much you'll pay to buy or hold a mutual fund, try FINRA's Fund Analyzer, https://tools.finra.org /fund_analyzer. The results can be eye-opening. For example, according to the FINRA's Fund Analyzer, over 10 years, the cost of investing $10,000 in one particular index fund will total $51.45. Investing the same amount in one actively managed stock fund that charges a commission and high fees will cost $1,528—almost 30 times more. Those costs are deducted from your account, which lowers the value of your investment.

How to find specific funds? A good starting point is to check the free and helpful resources provided by Morningstar, www.morningstar.com. On that site, you can screen for low-cost index funds or search for specific products, such as S&P 500 stock index funds, or a more narrowly focused offering, such as a fund that invests solely in health care stocks. The site also provides such useful data as how the fund's performance compares with the returns of similar funds, as well as the fund's fees, length of operation and the managers' profiles. But before you spring for a fund, read its prospectus—a brochure that describes the investment strategy and risks. Once you select a fund, phone or visit the website of the fund provider to open an account; you can also purchase funds and ETFs in a brokerage account.

PUTTING IT ALL TOGETHER

Building a portfolio of index funds is straightforward and smart: you will take advantage of these funds' low costs, broad diversification and, often, superior performance. You can cover all the asset classes by choosing six or seven index funds, one in each of the following categories:

- Stocks of large US companies (e.g., an S&P 500 index fund)
- Stocks of small US companies
- Stocks of non-US (foreign) companies
- Short-term bonds (that mature in 1 to 5 years)
- Intermediate-term bonds (that mature in 5 to 10 years)
- A money market fund (or CDs of varying maturities)

If you don't own your own home or a rental property, you can add a REIT to the list.

You may wish to supplement a set of index funds with one or more funds that reflect a particular interest. Many women are drawn to investing in socially responsible or ESG (environmental, social and governance) mutual funds. For more on ESG investing, see chapter 8.

USE AN ADVISOR?

It seems obvious to work with professionals (doctors, lawyers, financial advisors) whom you can trust to put your interests first. Yet many advisors are incentivized to recommend and sell investments and insurance that increase their own paycheck but may not be the best investments for you and your goals. Fiduciaries are bound, ethically and legally, to act in your best interests. When seeking someone to help you manage your finances, interview a few candidates and ask if they are fiduciaries and how they charge for advice.

Fee-only planners are fiduciaries who do not sell products; their compensation comes solely from client fees, such as a flat annual charge, a percentage of assets they manage or an hourly rate. For help finding a fee-only planner, check the websites of the National Association of Personal Financial Advisors (www.napfa.org), the Alliance of Comprehensive Planners (www.acplanners.org), the XY Planning Network (www.xyplanningnetwork.com) or the Garrett Planning Network (www.garrettplanningnetwork.com). The NAPFA website lists guidelines and questions to ask when searching for an advisor. Be sure to obtain a copy of the advisor's ADV registration form, which outlines the advisor's philosophy, fees and background.

8

THE ESG ATTRACTION

In August 2012, a year after she had retired, Melanie Lanctot was looking to invest some of her savings in a socially responsible way. For a third of her career, she'd been a program manager at the Maine Cancer Registry, discovering the extent to which smoking causes cancer. During that time, she was learning about the environmental hazards of burning fossil fuels.

So when Melanie visited a financial advisor that August, she knew what she wanted above all: to avoid tobacco and fossil fuel holdings.

The advisor recommended the Calvert Conservative Allocation Fund A. That's a fund of funds that invests in stocks, bonds and cash, with a tilt toward fixed income and a socially responsible investment mandate.

Melanie invested in that fund and watched her money grow, feeling doubly rewarded. As she says, "It's great to know that you can invest responsibly and still get a good return."

These days, ever more people seem to echo her sentiment. Socially responsible investing, now commonly called environmental, social and governance (ESG) investing, or sustainable investing, has been catching on fast, data show, amid the rising clamor over issues of mounting concern to the public. Issues range from climate change to gun violence, workers' rights, social justice and beyond. "To replace inaction by the government or business, citizens have been using what power they can to advance issues important to them," observes Elisabeth Kashner, director of fund research and analytics at FactSet, a financial data provider. Experts say the approach of investing in line with one's values strikes a chord with women.

"Women are friendlier to the concept that the way you invest matters," says Amy Domini, an ESG pioneer, who is founder and chair of Domini Impact Investments. Women tend to choose their investments with thought and care. ESG resonates, she says, because many women already have been dealing with societal issues through caregiving, their professions or their volunteer work.

Indeed, interest in ESG has been so strong among female clients of Karen Altfest, principal advisor at Altfest Personal Wealth Management, that she set up a lunch education session just for women. However, women aren't the only fans; she's finding that ESG "is attracting more and more men, and younger investors."

Data quantify how much ESG is growing: According to the US SIF Foundation, as of January 2020, sustainable investing assets in the United States reached $17.1 trillion—or 33 percent of total US assets under professional management. That $17.1 trillion was a 42 percent jump over 2018's level, stated the US SIF Foundation in its biennial *Report on US Sustainable and Impact Investing Trends 2020*.[1]

And investors apparently aren't done. Consider this outlook: "ESG-mandated assets in the United States could grow almost three times as fast as non-ESG-mandated assets to comprise half of all professionally managed investments by 2025," stated the firm of Deloitte, in a February 2020 report on ESG.[2]

To be sure, socially responsible/ESG/sustainable investing is not new; the first US mutual fund that was focused on investing in line with one's values debuted in the early 1970s. But like its name, the approach has evolved from its earliest days. Originally, it was aimed at avoiding socially undesirable companies and "sin" sectors—areas such as weaponry, gambling, adult entertainment and tobacco. Today, it's more about screening investments on ESG criteria—a host of issues, such as carbon emissions, workplace conditions, executive pay—along with financial factors. The idea: to find the best ESG investments while avoiding those with potentially costly ESG risks.

Shareholder engagement is another ESG component. That involves addressing social, environmental and governance issues with companies, and filing shareholder resolutions.

BACKGROUND

How did socially responsible/ESG investing evolve? Experts say the approach had early stirrings in the Vietnam War era. That's when some opponents of the war wanted to avoid investing in industries such as weapons producers and defense contractors. In the 1980s, visibility grew around the call to disinvest from companies doing business in South Africa while it practiced apartheid. But the big growth spurt was more recent, starting in the decade of the 2010s. It caught Wall Street's attention. And from there, a raft of new ESG-branded products and services emerged.

Through it all, Amy Domini has been a leading voice. It started with an idea: during her days as a stockbroker, from 1975 to 1979, she would call clients, pitching them the stock touted by her main office that day. But when some clients balked at certain suggestions, such as the stock of weapons makers' companies, she seized on a plan: on new clients' applications, she inserted a question about any investments the applicants wished to avoid. Intrigued by some clients' concerns, she began digging into ethical investing and then taught an adult education class on it.

In 1984, she published the groundbreaking book *Ethical Investing* and in 1989, she and partners started their own social research firm. A year later, Amy created the Domini 400 Social Index of 400 stocks, now known as the MSCI KLD 400 Social Index. Her first mutual fund debuted in 1991. And today, her firm, called Domini Impact Investments, offers five ESG mutual funds and engages in shareholder activism.

ESG investing now covers a broad landscape. Under that umbrella, you can find investments ranging from clean energy to low-income housing and community development to good corporate governance and beyond.

You can invest directly in projects or buy the stocks and bonds of organizations whose products or activities you support. But bear in mind that when you invest in a fund or buy stocks on the open market, you're not actually giving companies money. "Instead, you're buying stocks from a seller. It's not the same thing as corporate funding," notes FactSet's Elisabeth Kashner.

To wield more influence, she suggests engaging in corporate governance, which "is a more powerful way to influence a company." For instance, if you own stock, you can "vote your shares," typically at a company's annual meeting. And by binding with other shareholders, you can better promote your cause, she believes.

If you don't own individual companies' shares, you could invest in an ESG fund that has activist managers. By introducing and voting on resolutions at a company's annual meeting, these fund managers can push companies to make changes. And evidently, these actions are happening quite a lot: from 2018 through the first six months of 2020, 149 institutional investors and 56 investment managers led or co-led shareholder resolutions on ESG issues, according to the aforementioned US SIF Foundation report.[3]

RETURNS

But what about ESG's performance? Does investing according to your values shortchange you on returns, as some have feared? How well does ESG compare with the performance of standard investments?

Of course, performance depends on the period being measured. But that said, some observers hold that, at the very least, ESG appears to have been holding its own (as of this writing).

Consider the returns of the MSCI KLD 400 Social Index. MSCI describes it as a capitalization-weighted benchmark, which provides "exposure to companies with outstanding Environmental, Social and Governance (ESG) ratings, and excludes companies whose products have negative social or environmental impacts."[4]

According to data obtained from MSCI's website, www.msci.com, in 8 of the last 10 years ending December 31, 2020, the annual performance (gross returns in US dollars) of the MSCI KLD 400 beat the comparable performance of the MSCI USA Investable Market Index (IMI), which is an equity index of US large-, mid- and small-capitalization companies. (As of January 29, 2021, the MSCI KLD 400 had a 10-year annualized gross return of 13.68 percent, versus the comparable 13.56 percent for the MSCI USA IMI, MSCI data show.)[5]

HOW TO INVEST

So if you're intrigued by ESG, how do you proceed? What investing approach should you take?

Start by deciding on your tax strategy: Do you want to put ESG holdings into a taxable account or a tax-advantaged retirement account, such as an Individual Retirement Account (IRA) or your 401(k) plan account? Although many companies' 401(k) plans still don't have ESG options, you can—if your plan offers this feature—use the brokerage "window" option. This gives you access to investments options, including ESG offerings, outside your 401(k) plan.

Often individual ESG investors prefer to invest in stocks and bonds. But under the ESG heading, you also can find other options such as savings accounts and certificates of deposit.

You can pick investments on your own or use an ESG-style fund. Or you can hire a financial firm to create a portfolio for you. The latter, known as a separately managed account, often requires an investment of at least $250,000.

For many individuals, selecting individual stocks can be tricky. Beyond the sea of choices and normal due diligence needed to choose them, there's an extra dimension: figuring out which companies make good ESG investments. And that can get complicated, given the array of possible ESG factors.

Just a sampling of the possible conflicts to consider: Should you invest in a solar panel maker even if the company has few, or no, women or people of color as directors? Is everything to do with fossil fuels out of the question? What about nonpolluting businesses with black marks for financial irregularities? Or companies that score well on diversity and giving back to the community but create products in a sweatshop?

Also, how do you avoid "greenlining"? That's the practice in which a company provides false or misleading information about the ways it is protecting the environment through its policies and products.

One way to reduce the decisions you have to make—and get a diversified portfolio—is to use an ESG fund. That way, you let the fund manager sort through the ESG and financial criteria.

Certainly, there's no shortage of options today: you can find hundreds of ESG funds, which include mutual funds and exchange-traded funds (ETFs). Funds themselves widely range from those offering a broad swath of the market to those targeting a specific sector or theme or "niche" strategy, such as animal welfare, clean water or women's leadership.

WHERE TO LOOK

How to find ESG investments? Melanie Lanctot streamlined the process by consulting with a financial advisor. But you can research funds yourself: Get suggestions by reading the many articles on ESG or, as another source, checking the offerings of fund providers.

Among the resources on the internet is the nonprofit US SIF, the Forum for Sustainable and Responsible Investment; it provides free information on all sustainable-investment mutual funds and ETFs offered by US SIF's institutional member firms. You'll find data on the funds' type, asset size, performance, fees and more. You can access this offering at https://charts.ussif.org/mfpc. For information on separately managed accounts, visit https://charts.ussif.org/sam.

On its website, the nonprofit As You Sow (www.asyousow.org) provides transparency information on mutual funds and ETFs, including those with an ESG/sustainability mandate. Holdings in seven separate categories are flagged: fossil-free funds, deforestation-free funds, gender equality funds, weapons-free funds, gun-free funds, tobacco-free funds and prison-free funds. Locate this free offering on the site's Invest Your Values section.

DOING YOUR HOMEWORK

If you plan to invest in a particular fund, first read its prospectus. That report, which you can find online, contains such important information as who manages the fund, the fund's investment approach, its length of operation, its fees and its performance compared with that of a broad market index of that sector or subsector (such as small-cap stocks).

Check the fund's holdings. Be aware of any sectors (say, possibly technology, health care and others) that constitute a large portion of the fund. As experts point out, hefty exposure to a sector—especially if it's larger than its weighing in the index the fund measures itself against—could sway the fund's overall returns.

Beyond that, review the fund's stock holdings and see how well they reflect your interests. For instance, if you're worried about climate change, find out which, if any, energy companies' stocks the fund holds.

And be sure to check a fund's fees, since they will affect the return on your investment. Pay attention to a fund's expense ratio, which is the fee a fund company charges to operate a fund.

ACTIVE VERSUS PASSIVE FUNDS

Style-wise, you can choose between mutual funds and exchange-traded funds (ETFs).

Mutual funds are baskets of stocks and bonds that come in two flavors: actively managed and passively managed. "Actively" managed means their holdings are chosen at the discretion of a fund manager, while "passively" managed funds track a designated market index. In turn, ETFs are low-cost funds that are designed to track an index, and they trade like a stock on an exchange.

As a rule, index funds and ETFs will cost noticeably less—perhaps by as much as two-thirds or more—than actively managed mutual funds, depending on the funds. But that expense ratio doesn't need to sway your choice. In fact, actively managed funds could be good picks if they've had strong long-term performance.

ESG RATINGS

Want ESG ratings on potential investments? Today, you can get them from an evidently growing array of providers. Two online resources to consider include MSCI ESG Ratings and the Morningstar Sustainability Rating.

MSCI ESG Research offers free and publicly available ESG ratings of public companies and funds. These offerings assess individual companies and funds on a "AAA" to "CCC" scale according to their exposure to ESG risks and how well they manage them relative to peers. On the internet, you'll find MSCI ESG Ratings of funds at www.msci.com/esg-fund-ratings and the ESG ratings of companies at www.msci.com/esg-ratings.

The Morningstar Sustainability Rating applies to funds. Its process involves using ratings from Sustainalytics to determine how well the companies held in a fund manage their ESG risks and opportunities. With that score, Morningstar then rates funds versus their peers, on a one-to-five scale (using globes), with five globes being the highest sustainability rating. To access this free offering, visit a fund's page on Morningstar.com, then click on the portfolio tab and scroll down to find the fund's rating. To see the full methodology, you can go to https://www.morningstar.com/research/signature.

HOW MUCH SHOULD YOU INVEST IN ESG?

That may depend on such factors as your familiarity and experience with social investing. Karen Altfest says most of her firm's clients using ESG invest a percentage—but not all—of their investable assets in ESG.

However, you can create a whole portfolio of ESG holdings. For instance, you could buy a broad market stock or bond fund to serve as the core of your stock or bond holdings and then add funds targeting specific market areas, such as international stocks, small-capitalization stocks, funds with specific types of bonds, and funds targeting a niche, such as clean water or advancing women in leadership, experts say.

Here's one possible allocation for your stocks: Say you want to have 60 percent of your portfolio in ESG-designated stocks. In that case, you might put 60 percent of that total in US funds. Of that, about two-thirds could be in large-capitalization and one-third in small- to mid-cap stock funds. You could invest the remaining 40 percent in ESG funds targeting international or emerging markets investments and perhaps some specific niche themes.

And when picking funds, try getting some extra bang: choose fund managers that actively engage with companies to promote ESG issues.

And as for ESG bond funds? These are attractive if you're seeking lower risk than with stock funds or want to balance your portfolio. Among the types of bonds to consider: US government securities, municipal bonds, corporate bonds and non-US bonds. So-called green bonds are another possibility; these finance projects designed to have a positive effect on climate and the environment.

DON'T JUST INVEST AND FORGET ABOUT IT

After you invest, be sure to monitor the portfolio at least once per quarter to ensure that it's adhering to practices you expected. To keep up, read a company's disclosures, including its annual report and fund manager's reports, its blogs and its quarterly performance data. Some fund providers publish such helpful information as the carbon emissions of the companies in their portfolios and/or how much low-income housing was created. If you can't find at least an annual impact statement from your fund providers, contact them. Find out how they are ensuring that their investments are indeed ESG.

And what if you want to do more with your money to advance social issues? Consider opening a savings account or buying a certificate of deposit (CD) at a community development bank or credit union. These institutions help communities in low- and moderate-income areas. Supporting them means helping their communities. To explore this concept further, visit www.cdfi.org, the website of the CDFI Coalition.

9

SAFEGUARDING YOUR ASSETS

Sad to say, risks to your financial security can come at you from many angles: scams, identity theft, lawsuits and market plunges, to name a few common ones. But in the case of Brooke Astor, the renowned socialite and philanthropist, the threat came from her own son, Anthony Marshall.

Brooke's story is a harrowing account of fraud and elder abuse. As her grandson, Philip Marshall (Anthony's son), recounts, the crimes occurred after Brooke was over 100 years old and was suffering from Alzheimer's disease. Philip noticed an increasingly worrisome situation: by around 2005, his multimillionaire grandmother was living in a cold, dirty New York apartment. She was emaciated and visibly frightened.

He decided to intervene.

On a January evening in 2006, Philip arrived at his grandmother's New York City residence after his father—who was using part of this Upper East Side co-op as his office—had left for the night. Speaking with two of Brooke's nurses, Philip learned the horrifying details: Anthony had fired some of Brooke's trusted staff, was depriving his mother of comfort and was preventing her friends from visiting her. In addition, he had brought in lawyers to get his mentally ailing mother to sign legal documents.

Over the next few months, Philip worked with Brooke's staff and friends to map a plan, which led to his filing for her guardianship. "It was the only card I could play," says Philip, since his father had a power-of-attorney for Brooke Astor. Further legal actions ensued. Eventually, these led to a criminal trial in which Anthony Marshall was convicted of 14 out of 16 counts of defrauding and stealing from his mother. (A lawyer who had done estate planning for Brooke was convicted on 5 counts of criminal activity in the case.)

Brooke spent her final year—she died in 2007—living peacefully at her home in Westchester County, New York, says Philip, who went on to be a champion against elder abuse, with a cause-based campaign called Beyond Brooke. But her story continues to resonate, warning everyone of the need to protect themselves. Although the wealthy may be prime targets for fraud, experts warn that anyone can lose money, often in unexpected ways.

How does this happen? What common risks loom over your financial picture? Some familiar culprits include accidents, lawsuits, market plunges and scams. And for single women, certain risks, such as indulging adult children, may exist close to home.

For widows, bankrolling their adult children could be tempting. "Emotions may be overwhelming these women. Potentially, they could be frightened, lonely and want their family around. And they may be managing their finances for the first time," says financial advisor Evelyn Zohlen, president and founder of Inspired Financial and 2020 chair of the Financial Planning Association. If their adult children ask them for money—perhaps because they're jobless or living beyond their means—these mothers might want to comply. But by doing so, she says, "They could strain their own finances—and at a time when they may not have the option to go to work."

Divorcées could face a variation on the risk. For example, if they feel guilty about the divorce, they might try to assuage their feelings by giving money to their young adult kids.

"But don't start down that path," advises Evelyn Zohlen. "Have boundaries. Allocate money for gifting in your basic budget—perhaps creating one line in the budget for family members' gifts and another for charitable donations. Set an upper limit for both types of gifting, say, $10,000 for the year, and stick to it," she says.

And if you're headed toward the altar, heed this advice: plan to keep your premarital money in your own name after you wed. This way, if you should later divorce, your own funds would not be counted as marital assets to be divided up, points out Janice Cackowski, partner at Centry Financial Advisors. Similarly, goods or funds you inherit should be kept in your name, even after you marry, to ensure they are not included in any future divorce settlement.

DISABILITY PROTECTION

For singles, it's a must. If you're not retired, and you depend on your earnings, consider what would happen if injuries or ill health kept you from working. The possibilities aren't remote: according to the Council for Disability Awareness (CDA), before normal retirement age, more than one in four of today's 20-year-olds can expect to be out of work at least a year due to a disabling condition.[1] Without an income stream from work, you could struggle to pay bills and potentially exhaust your savings. The prospect is even more worrisome if you're self-employed: if you couldn't work, you'd not only forgo your income but would also lack access to money-saving, employer-sponsored benefits.

As one lifeline, disability insurance (DI) provides a portion of your salary when you can't work. Yet according to a CDA survey, 52 percent of single female workers ages 20 to 65 have no disability insurance, and of those who do have it, only 55 percent say they have enough.[2]

Coverage Options

If you're lucky, you can get the coverage through your employer. According to the US Bureau of Labor Statistics (BLS), in 2019, 40 percent of civilian workers had access to short-term disability insurance, and 34 percent could get long-term coverage. Employers who offer disability insurance pay the full cost of it for most workers, according to the BLS.

If the coverage isn't available through work, seek an individual DI policy from an insurance company. The cost will run you about 1 percent to 3 percent of your annual gross income. "The trick is to buy it when you're young and healthy so that you'll pay closer to the 1 percent," says Carol Harnett, president of the CDA. As another possible source, many professional associations offer members the opportunity to buy a group disability plan. In that case, the member would pay all of her premium, she adds.

Typically, short-term policies provide about three months of coverage, while long-term plans kick in after that—at about three months.

To be sure, the Social Security Administration provides disability insurance for people who have paid their FICA (Federal Insurance Contributions Act) tax for a stipulated period. But qualifying for this benefit can be tough.

If you're on a group disability plan, your insurer will help you apply for Social Security Disability Insurance (SSDI). If you do get SSDI and you're on a group long-term disability plan, your insurer will deduct your Social Security benefit from the amount it pays you. But if you have an individual disability policy, the insurer may not be willing to help you apply for SSDI (in which case, you'd apply on your own) and may not deduct SSDI from its payout to you.

Note: Workers' Compensation covers inability to work due to a disability that is directly job-related. If your accident or illness occurs at work, report it immediately to your employer and fill out a workers' compensation claim. Obtain the form from your employer or your state's workers' compensation board.

UMBRELLA PROTECTION

But what if a risk to your assets seems to spring from out of nowhere? Say you're driving in a blinding downpour. As you round a 90-degree curve in the road, you swerve into the opposite lane and crash into a car with two passengers. The injured passengers each sue you for $1 million.

Or you host a pool party at your home, and a guest falls into the shallow end of the pool, cracking his skull. His family hits you with a massive lawsuit.

How can you financially survive such catastrophes?

Many experts recommend having personal umbrella insurance. "It's the first line of defense in all asset protection strategies," says Joseph Weiss, insurance specialist at Bruce Gendelman Insurance Services.

Its benefits extend liability coverage beyond the limits of your homeowners, automobile, renters and boaters insurance. It covers injuries and damage you unintentionally cause others and their property with your car or boat, or accidents that occur at your home—including dog bites. It also covers you for slander, libel and even mental anguish.

This protection does not apply to your injuries and damage to your property. But it does cover your legal fees in case you get sued.

Umbrella insurance typically costs between $150 and $300 a year, reports Penny Gusner, senior consumer analyst at Insure.com, an independent consumer insurance website. Policies start at $1 million of coverage and rise in increments of $1 million.

To buy umbrella insurance, you'll need to already have a specified amount of underlying coverage, which for many people would be homeowners and auto insurance. While insurance companies' rules can differ, typically you need to be carrying at least $300,000 of liability coverage on your home and auto policies in order to purchase an umbrella. Thus, if you bought a $1 million umbrella policy, you'd have a total of $1.3 million of liability coverage, says Joseph Weiss.

Financial planner Bruce Colin of Rancho Palos Verdes, California, strongly encourages people to "get this insurance. It's relatively inexpensive compared with the protection it affords." He particularly recommends it for people who own a house, condominium, townhouse or car.

But bear in mind: even if you incur a liability, not all your assets are likely to be at risk. Depending on your state's regulations, your primary residence may be protected in part or in full from a liability lawsuit. And your 401(k) assets are shielded.

INVESTMENT PROTECTIONS

Diversifying Your Portfolio

If you're smart, you've been saving for retirement by dutifully putting 10 percent or more of your wages into a 401(k) or IRAs. But what if these invested assets suddenly shrank in value, battered by a market crash? How do you protect your savings—your financial future—from such havoc?

You could park savings in cash, in such safe instruments as certificates of deposit (CDs). But you'd be unlikely to see much asset appreciation.

The better solution is to diversify investments, using a mix of fixed income securities, stocks, ultrasafe cash and possibly real estate. This way, if one asset class drops in value, others may hold steady or rise, since typically investment classes don't all move in the same direction.

In turbulent times, the process can be especially reassuring: "Market fluctuations—while never pleasant—are generally bearable if your portfolio is properly diversified, calibrated to the amount of risk you can tolerate—and designed to fit your long-term needs," says Kimberly Foss, founder and president of Empyrion Wealth Management.

"I construct portfolios for clients that combine investments for future growth—typically stocks and stock mutual funds—with those that feature less volatility and more safety," she says. The latter might include "government and high-quality corporate bonds and bond mutual funds." This design can give women "the investment growth needed to ensure their funds will last . . . and that provides income over the long term."

Annuities

But what if you have no stomach for rocky, unpredictable markets? Or you want some guaranteed income coming in, especially in retirement?

In those cases, buying an annuity could be a solution.

By definition, an annuity is a contract with an insurance company. You invest qualified (pre-tax) or nonqualified (after-tax) dollars with an insurer and at a specified time, frequently in retirement, you get back a lump sum or a regular income stream that is often for life. Annuities come in numerous variations within the main categories of variable or fixed, and deferred or immediate (payout).

Some people buy them to shield their assets from market losses, some to protect their principal and some to obtain guaranteed income.

Many forms of annuities have been criticized for their head-scratching complexity and their commissions and fees. And in most cases, your annuity contract will lock up a portion of your money in it until the contract expires. Annuities—although not all types—can impose a surrender charge of up to 10 percent of the money you invested if you reclaim your annuity funds early.

But on the plus side, if you're seeking a guaranteed or a pension-like payout, some types of annuities can be appealing. In particular, the single premium immediate annuity (SPIA) can be attractive to those who want a straightforward, uncomplicated income stream without fancy clauses and if-then scenarios. With the SPIA, you give an insurance company a lump sum and you get back—frequently starting a month later—a specified, guaranteed income stream. Often you buy the SPIA when you're in or near retirement, and the payouts supplement your retirement income, typically for the rest of your life. One place to find an online SPIA quote calculator is Immediate annuities.com (www.immediateannuities.com), an online annuity brokerage firm.

SPIA payments include a portion of your principal plus a small amount of interest. The latter tends to be slightly higher than that of a CD or money market instrument. Payouts are based on such factors as your age, current interest rates and expected length of payments. Essentially, the younger you are, the lower your regular payout, says Ariel Stern, COO of Immediateannuities.com. That's because younger buyers are likely to receive SPIA payments over a longer period than older buyers.

Among their attractions, SPIAs are predictable and can help ease the fear of running out of money in retirement, Ariel points out. They also have no surrender charges.

Bear in mind, however, that once you make your SPIA investment, it is locked in; typically, you can't get your money back. What's more, payments from "single life only" SPIAs—the type single people commonly prefer—end with your life.

AVOIDING FRAUDSTERS

These vultures search relentlessly for prey. To steal your money and identity, they may target you by phone, email, texts, advertisements and other means. In 2019, the Consumer Sentinel Network of the Federal Trade Commission (FTC) received 3.2 million reports of fraud. According to the FTC, imposter scams led the pack of frauds that year. Victims lost more than $667 million to these scammers, the Commission reported. These thieves frequently pretended to be representing the government, a business, a romantic interest, or a family member needing money.

Experts say some scammers tie up your computer and then request gift cards as payment to fix the problem; some urge you to "call back now" to obtain a refund. Indeed, among the blizzard of scams during the coronavirus-triggered recession of 2020: fraudsters stole people's identity and then applied for unemployment compensation in the victims' name.

Evidently, adults of all ages can be targets. In an October 2020 report to Congress, the FTC stated that in 2019, as in 2018, those age 60 and older were less likely to report losing money to fraud than younger adults were. But the amounts lost by those age 60-plus were, in fact, much higher—with the largest losses, a median individual forfeiture of $1,600, reported among people age 80 and older. In a press release, the FTC said that, among older adults, online shopping scams were the most frequent type of fraud, while romance scams produced the largest dollar losses.

Evidently, thieves can be highly resourceful. For instance, they can learn the names of your grandchildren, perhaps from your social media postings. Armed with this information, they call you, impersonating one of your grandchildren and asking for money because they're in trouble or have an emergency.

Or a thief might find you on a dating site or "friend" you on social media. From there, the problems mount. Over time, the person keeps in close touch and professes deepening affection. You become convinced that this is true love. Once you're hooked, the scammer launches into a sob story and broadly hints at a need for financial help or asks for money outright. If you comply, the thief continues to ask for money until you catch on and stop payments.

Indeed, "People have lost up to millions of dollars to someone they thought loves them," says Kristin Judge, CEO of Cybercrime Support Network.

How should you protect yourself? Kristin Judge offers three "golden rules" for avoiding scammers: Slow it down. Spot check. Stop! Don't send.[3]

- **Slow it down.** No matter how urgent-sounding the request for money is, don't react immediately. Take time to ask questions.
- **Spot check.** Verify the identity of callers or emailers. If the contacts are seeking your personal information, get their phone number and tell them you'll call them back. If a caller claims to be a family member, contact another member of your family to verify the information you received from the caller.
- **Stop! Don't send.** Ignore unexpected requests for money— especially from unverified sources. For instance, if someone calls to say you've won the lottery but need to send $300 to have your winnings processed, it's most likely a scam. The same applies to a request for payment via a gift card.

Other safeguards experts recommend:

- Don't immediately give money to solicitors claiming to help victims of natural disasters. Instead, use the website of a charity to make donations, says John Gill, vice president-education, Association of Certified Fraud Examiners.

- If an organization emails you claiming to be your bank or other firm, check the sender's email address. If that organization's name isn't on the email's address (such as smith@ABank.com), delete the message, John Gill adds.
- Get a credit freeze, also called security freeze. According to the Consumer Financial Protection Bureau (CFPB), this move "prevents prospective creditors from accessing your credit file."

As the CFPB explains, "creditors typically won't offer you credit if they can't access your credit reporting file." Thus, implementing a security freeze, also called a credit freeze, prevents you or others—including identity thieves—from opening accounts in your name.

You can freeze and, as needed, unfreeze your credit record for free at the three nationwide credit reporting firms, Equifax, Experian and TransUnion. It's also wise to check your credit reports annually from each of these firms at www.annualcreditreport.com.

If you become a victim of a scam, report the incident to the FTC at https://reportfraud.ftc.gov. For help reporting and recovering from identity theft, visit the FTC's site, www.identitytheft.gov.

10

TAXING MATTERS

Unless you are expecting a tax refund, you may hate April 15. Of course, that's the day federal taxes are due. And it hits single people especially hard: overall, unwed people pay more in federal taxes than married couples do on the same income because of the current tax structure. Hopefully, someday soon, Washington will correct this inequity. But for now, it's crucial to recognize and seize any opportunities to cut your tax bill. After all, trimming $100 off your taxes is equivalent to getting a $135 bonus at work.

How to proceed? It starts with being aware of federal tax policies and how they can work for you. The implications are far-reaching: almost every outlay involves your taxes in some way. Do you rent or buy a house? Should you choose health insurance with a high or low deductible? Are Roth IRAs more attractive than 401(k) retirement plans? Understanding how income taxes affect you—from the rates you pay to the ways to pare your tax bill—helps determine the amount of personal spending money you have. (Although this chapter addresses only federal income taxes, 43 states and many cities and school districts also impose income taxes. Learn more about the tax rules and rates in your state on the USA.gov website [https://www.usa .gov/state-taxes].)

FEDERAL INCOME TAX RATES

Since the United States has a progressive income tax system, the higher your income, the higher your tax rate. But not all income is taxed at the same rate unless you earn $9,950 or less (in 2021). For tax purposes, income is grouped into brackets, each of which has its own tax rate. Only income that exceeds the highest amount in the previous bracket is taxed at a higher rate. The breakdown for a person filing as Single on a 2021 tax return is shown below.

Table 10.1. Federal Income Tax Brackets—Filing Single (2021)

Tax Rate	Taxable Income (after Deductions)
10%	Up to $9,950
12%	$9,951 to $40,525
22%	$40,526 to $86,375
24%	$86,376 to $164,925
32%	$164,926 to $209,425
35%	$209,426 to $523,600
37%	$523,601 or more

Source: Internal Revenue Service.

Take the hypothetical case of a 40-year-old office manager—we'll call her Talia—who earns $50,550. After taking the standard deduction, her taxable income has been reduced to $38,000. According to current tax laws, $9,950 of the $38,000 falls in the 10 percent tax bracket while the remaining $28,050 falls in the 12 percent tax bracket. The calculation of her $4,361 tax bill is shown in table 10.2.

Table 10.2. Calculation of Talia's Federal Income Tax

Tax Rate	Taxable Income after Deductions	Taxes Owed
10%	$9,950	$995
12%	Remaining $28,050	$3,366
Total		**$4,361**
Average rate: 11.5%		

Note: Talia earns $50,550 and takes the $12,550 standard deduction. Her taxable income is $38,000.

Let's say Talia gets a $3,000 bonus, boosting her income to $53,550 or a taxable income of $41,000. Although delighted with the added income, Talia is concerned this windfall will bump her into a higher tax bracket and she will be financially worse off than before she got the bonus. But not so: only the last $475 of Talia's income falls into the higher 22 percent tax bracket. The calculation of Talia's taxes with her bonus is shown in table 10.3.

Table 10.3. Calculation of Talia's Federal Income Tax with a $3,000 Bonus

Tax Rate	Taxable Income after Deductions	Taxes Owed
10%	$9,950	$995
12%	($40,525–$9,950) $30,575	$3,669
22%	Remaining $475	$105
Total		**$4,769**
Average rate: 11.6%		

Note: Including her $3,000 bonus, Talia earns $53,550 and takes the $12,550 standard deduction. Her taxable income is $41,000.

Talia paid $408 in federal taxes on her $3,000 bonus. Her "effective" or average tax rate is 11.6 percent, only a smidge over her pre-bonus effective rate of 11.5 percent.

As of this writing, investment income such as profits, known as capital gains, and stock dividends are taxed at a lower rate than wages are. Capital gains are the profits from the sale of assets such as stocks, mutual funds, bonds or real estate. You must own the asset for at least a year and a day before selling to qualify for the capital gains tax rate on the profit.

Capital gains have their own tax brackets. In 2021, if you file as Single and your taxable income is lower than $40,400, you will pay no tax on your capital gains and qualified dividends. Your capital gains rate is zero. If your income is between $40,400 and $445,850, your capital gains rate is 15 percent and, at higher levels of income, your capital gains are taxed at 20 percent, under rules in effect in early 2021.

Let's say our hypothetical office manager, Talia, purchased a few shares of stock for $1,000 a couple of years ago. If she sells the stock—now worth $1,500—her profit of $500 is taxed at capital gains rates.

With no bonus, her taxable income will be $38,000 plus the $500 profit. Talia will owe no federal taxes on her stock profit because her total taxable income is under $40,400. (She may owe state income taxes on the gain.) If Talia scored twice and received both a $3,000 bonus and a $500 profit on her stock sale, the extra income would bump her into the 22 percent tax bracket, and part of her stock profits would be taxed. A comparison of Talia's tax bill after she sold the stock—with and without a bonus—is shown in table 10.4.

Table 10.4. Comparison of Talia's Federal Income Tax after Stock Sale without and with Bonus

	Without Bonus	With Bonus
Taxable income	$38,500	$41,500
Total tax	$4,361	$4,844
Tax bracket	12.0%	22.0%
Average tax rate	11.3%	11.7%

Note that Talia's average tax rate on her salary plus the $500 capital gain (but no bonus) is 11.3 percent—lower than her average rate without the capital gain (11.5 percent), as shown in table 10.2. The average tax rate is the percentage of your taxable income you pay in taxes. Talia's income increased when she added the $500 capital gain, but because she paid no tax on the profit, her average rate declined.

YOUR TAX STATUS AND CLAIMING DEPENDENTS

As a single person, you may file one of three ways, depending on your situation: Single, Head of Household or Qualifying Widow. Choosing the wrong filing status can cost thousands of dollars in extra taxes.

Qualifying Widow status allows you to keep the benefits of Married Filing Jointly for two years after your spouse passes away. Tax laws generally favor married couples, so this can be a significant tax break. To be eligible, you must have a dependent child or stepchild living in your home for which you pay at least half the expenses. You must be unmarried during the first two years of widowhood, and in the year your spouse died, you must have filed a joint tax return.

For tax purposes, Head of Household status is also better than filing as Single, because the standard deduction is larger and the tax brackets are more generous. To qualify for Head of Household status, you must be unmarried on the last day of the year (or be considered unmarried because you lived apart from your spouse from July 1 through December 31), you must pay more than half of the expenses of keeping up your home and a "qualifying person" must have lived with you for more than half the year.

A "qualifying person" can be either a qualifying child or a qualifying relative. A qualifying child is generally your son, daughter, grandchild, sibling or niece or nephew who is younger than 19 or, if a student, younger than 24, or is disabled (at any age). Qualifying children are required to live with you—or be away at college—for at least half the year and must not provide more than half of their own support.

A qualifying relative either lives with you for the entire year or is a relative such as a child, parent or sibling. Qualifying relatives' income must be less than $4,300 (in 2021), and you must have provided more than half of their support.

So, if you claim a child on your tax return, you should be able to file as Head of Household, right? It depends. Take the hypothetical case of two unmarried sisters who each earn $45,000—we'll call them Marisa and Gloria. Marisa's 10-year-old daughter lives with her, allowing Marisa to file as Head of Household which reduces her taxes. Gloria's 12-year-old son lives with her ex-husband, so Gloria does not qualify for Head of Household; her only option is filing as Single. However, as part of the divorce settlement, Gloria's ex-husband signed form 8332, allowing Gloria to claim their son on her tax return.

Thus both Marisa and Gloria get the maximum Child Tax Credit of $3,000 (in 2021). This reduces their taxes on a dollar-for-dollar basis.

But what if this credit is larger than your tax bill? The good news is the credit is "refundable." That means if the credit is larger than the taxes owed, it would not only wipe out your tax bill but also provide you with a refund for the difference. As shown in table 10.5, Gloria's Child Tax Credit offsets $3,000 of her $3,695 tax bill, reducing her tax bill to $695. In contrast, Marisa won't owe any taxes and, on top of that benefit, will get a $140 refund. Thus, Marisa scores in two ways:

Table 10.5. Comparison of Marisa's and Gloria's 2021 Taxes

	Marisa	Gloria
Filing status	Head of Household	Single
Number of dependents	I	I
Income	$45,000	$45,000
Standard deduction	$18,800	$12,550
Taxable income	$26,200	$32,450
Regular taxes	$2,860	$3,695
Child Tax Credit	$3,000	$3,000
Total tax with credit	**$140 refund**	**$695 owed**
Tax bracket	**12%**	**12%**

Note: Taxes were calculated using the income tax calculator on the Calculator.net website.

as Head of Household, she had a lower tax bill than Gloria, and could also claim the Child Tax Credit.

Parents are not the only taxpayers who can qualify to file as Head of Household. If you provide more than half of your parent's support and can claim them as a dependent, you can file as Head of Household even if your parent doesn't live with you. This can be a boon if you are paying the cost of your mother's nursing home, for example.

WIDOWS AND TAXES

Among the many upheavals you face after the loss of your spouse is the change in your tax status. When you are widowed, your tax filing status depends on your circumstances, and there are several choices:

- In the year of your spouse's death, you are permitted to file as either Married Filing Jointly or Married Filing Separately.
- In subsequent years, if you have no dependents and you have not remarried, you will file as Single.
- If you claim a child or stepchild as a dependent, you may be able to file as Qualifying Widow for two years after your spouse's death. When your eligibility to file as Qualifying Widow expires, you switch either to Head of Household, if you have a qualified dependent, or to Single.

For many widows, their house is their biggest asset. When deciding whether to keep or sell a home, weigh the tax implications. If you no longer wish to keep your home, you may do better tax-wise selling it within two years after your spouse's death. You will not be taxed on up to $500,000 of profit as long as you meet three criteria: you and your spouse lived in the house as your principal residence for two of the past five years; either or both of you owned the home for the same time period; and neither has taken advantage of this benefit over the past two years.

But what if you wish to keep your home for more than two years after your spouse dies? In that case, your tax break will shrink. Under current rules, the IRS allows only $250,000 of the profit to be tax-free after that two-year period.

After your spouse dies, you also get a tax break when you inherit other assets, such as stocks, bonds and mutual funds. Investments held solely by your spouse, or your spouse's share of a joint investment account, receive a stepped-up basis. Here's how it works: Under current rules, if your spouse bought stock for $5,000 and it appreciated to $25,000 by the time your spouse died, the IRS calculates your taxable profit on anything earned above $25,000, not the original $5,000. Thus, if the stock appreciates to $35,000 when you sell it, you will owe taxes only on $10,000 of capital gains.

IRAs and other retirement plans inherited from your spouse are taxed differently from other investments. If you are the sole beneficiary of your deceased spouse's IRA (traditional, Roth or SEP) or retirement plan such as a 401(k), you may roll over the account to your own IRA. (If you are not the only beneficiary, your share must be split off by December 31 of the year after your spouse died.) A Roth IRA or Roth 401(k) assets will be rolled over to your own Roth IRA; move a traditional IRA or 401(k) plan to your own traditional IRA.

With traditional IRAs, you can make withdrawals at any time, but you will owe taxes on the withdrawal—and a 10 percent penalty on it if you are younger than 59½. (Taxes on Roth IRAs are explained later in this chapter.) Currently, when you reach age 72, you must start taking Required Minimum Distributions (RMDs) annually from all IRAs except Roth IRAs.

Quick Tip: If you are younger than age 59½ when your spouse dies, it may be better to keep your late spouse's IRA in a separate account as an Inherited IRA. Withdrawals from an Inherited IRA avoid the 10 percent penalty that usually applies if you are under age 59½. And if you don't need the money now, you can delay taking RMDs from the Inherited IRA until the year your spouse would have turned 72. If the inherited account is from your spouse, you can move money out of an Inherited IRA into your own IRA any time, but it's a one-way street: you can't roll that money back into an Inherited IRA.

DIVORCÉES AND TAXES

Too often, the tax consequences of a divorce are ignored in the heat of the moment. Yet many of the decisions made while negotiating the divorce—from how the assets are divided, to who can claim children, to who pays alimony and/or child support—will affect your tax bill for many years. Knowing the tax consequences will help you negotiate a better settlement.

If you are divorced and have no dependents on December 31, you will file Single for that tax year. If a qualifying dependent lives with you for at least six months of the year, you can claim Head of Household status if you are unmarried (or you lived apart from your spouse for the last six months of the year) and you pay for more than half the cost of keeping a home.

The custodial parent—the parent with whom the child lives the greater number of nights—generally files as Head of Household. If you are the custodial parent, you can preserve Head of Household status but allow your former spouse to claim your child as a dependent (as Gloria's former spouse did in our example earlier in the chapter).

As the custodial parent, you will keep the Child and Dependent Care Tax Credit and the Earned Income Tax Credit (if you're eligible), but if you allow your former spouse to claim your child, you will give away the Child Tax Credit and college credits. (See "Tax Credits," below.) On its website, the IRS (www.irs.gov) provides tools for determining your tax filing status and whom you can claim as a dependent.

Quick Tip: If you are divorced and your child attends college, you may be better off claiming your child on your own tax return rather than giving your ex-spouse that benefit. The American Opportunity college tax credit can reduce your tax bill by as much as $2,500, no matter who pays the college expenses, as long as you claim the student on your tax return.

Child support payments are tax-free income to the person who receives them and are not deductible by the person who pays. If your divorce was finalized after December 31, 2018, the same goes for alimony payments. If you were divorced before that date, you will owe taxes on alimony payments you receive, and you can deduct alimony you pay.

Divorce decrees often specify a transfer of all or part of one spouse's pension or 401(k) plan to the other spouse. This split is done via a Qualified Domestic Relations Order, or QDRO. The amount that is withdrawn from one spouse's retirement plan is typically deposited in the recipient's IRA although, in some cases, the money can stay in the retirement plan under the recipient's name.

SINGLES AND TAXES

Many of the tax strategies available to married couples (such as filing jointly vs. separately or funding a spousal IRA for a stay-at-home spouse) do not exist for singles. Yet there are a few bright spots in the tax rules for single filers. The $10,000 ceiling on deducting state and local taxes and the $750,000 mortgage limit (see "Tax Deductions," below) are identical for a single taxpayer or married couple. Thus a married couple's combined deductions have to fit under those thresholds, while a single taxpayer gets the full deduction herself.

Additional Medicare taxes kick in when a single taxpayer earns more than $200,000. Two taxpayers who are married do not get twice that limit; they will pay the extra taxes if their joint income is above $250,000.

An unmarried taxpayer who shares a home with her partner may be able to claim her partner as a dependent—as long as the partner earns less than $4,300 (in 2021) and doesn't pay more than half of the household expenses. And if you are raising a child together, it may make sense for the higher earner to claim the child and file as Head of Household.

Quick Tip: If only one partner has enough deductible expenses to itemize (as described below), that partner could make all the charitable donations for the household, in order to increase her deductions. The other partner can take the standard deduction—and chip in more for nondeductible expenses to even things out.

TAX DEDUCTIONS

The majority of tax filers—over 86 percent in 2019, according to estimates by the Tax Foundation[1]—take the standard deduction. The alternative—itemizing tax deductions—is worthwhile only if deductible expenses total more than the amount of the standard deduction. The standard deduction in 2021 is $12,550 for a single filer, $18,800 for head of household status and $25,100 for a qualifying widow. If you are 65 or older, you add $1,700 to your standard deduction if you file as single or head of household and $1,350 if you are a qualifying widow.

Common Deductible Expenses

Mortgage Interest. The tax laws tend to favor homeowners—although that is only one consideration when deciding to buy or rent. In the early twentieth century, Congress decided to encourage home ownership by allowing taxpayers to deduct the interest on their mortgage from their taxable income. As a result, a homeowner with a mortgage paid lower taxes than a renter with the same income. Lured in part by this tax break, millions of Americans bought homes financed with mortgage loans.

You can deduct interest on a mortgage up to $750,000 (or $1 million if your mortgage was signed before December 15, 2017) as long as you used the loan money to buy, build or substantially remodel your home. The deduction applies both to your principal home and to a vacation home as long as your combined mortgage amount doesn't exceed those limits. To get this tax benefit, however, you must itemize your tax deductions.

Another plus for homeowners: you can get a tax break when you sell your home at a profit. If you have owned and lived in your home for two of the past five years before selling, your profit is tax-free—up to $250,000 for a single person. And it's not a once-in-a-lifetime tax break; each time you sell a home you are entitled to exclude up to $250,000 profit as long as you meet the requirements.

Taxes. If you itemize, currently, you can deduct only $10,000 for such taxes as:

- State, city and school district income taxes (federal income taxes are not deductible)
- Property taxes on real estate you own, including your home
- Personal property taxes on cars, boats and other vehicles

Sales tax you paid during the year is deductible if that amount is larger than income taxes paid to your state, city and school district combined. You can keep track of the sales tax you paid during the year or use the calculator on the IRS website to estimate how much you paid, based on your income.

Medical Expenses. Doctor and dentist bills, hospital bills and the cost of eyeglasses and prescriptions you pay out of pocket are all tax deductible if they total more than 7.5 percent of your adjusted gross income and if your total deductible expenses exceed the standard deduction. Premiums for health insurance are deductible unless they are paid directly from your paycheck.

Quick Tip: If you itemize, you can deduct medical expenses paid for a dependent or for someone who would have qualified as your dependent if the person had not earned more than $4,300 (in 2021)—such as an adult child living at home. For example, if your 28-year-old son is living at home and earned $5,000 at a part-time job, you may be able to deduct his health insurance premiums, dentist bills and other medical expenses on your own tax return.

Charitable Deductions. If you don't itemize your deductions, you do not receive a tax break for your charitable deductions with the exception of up to $300 in donations you can deduct without itemizing. But all is not lost. Other ways to claim a tax break from your charitable donations include:

- Clean out your closets. If you are close to itemizing, the amount you can deduct by donating used clothing and other items may tip the total over the standard deduction threshold. Keep track of every article of clothing, piece of furniture or any other item you donate. Take a picture of your donations and use a guide supplied by the charity or available on the Goodwill or Salvation Army website to assign a value to each item. Get a dated receipt from the charity and attach it to your list and photo for your records.
- Itemize every other year. If you typically take the standard deduction, you may have enough deductions to itemize if you increase your charitable donations in the current year and/or pay two years' worth of property taxes in one year. Then, in the following year, because you have prepaid your property taxes and donations, take the standard deduction.
- Make a contribution to a charity from your IRA. This tax benefit is called a Qualified Charitable Distribution. If you are 70½ or older, ask the company that holds your IRA to send you a check made out to a specific charity. This money comes out of your IRA tax-free; you don't have to itemize to get this tax break.
- Create your own charitable account, called a donor-advised fund. You can set one up with a financial institution (such as Fidelity or Schwab) or with your local community foundation. Fund the account by contributing cash or shares of investments. Then direct the company managing the fund to send checks to the charities of your choice. Your contribution of cash or securities is deductible in the year you make it. And you pay no capital gains tax on the profits of shares of stocks or mutual funds you contribute.

TAX CREDITS

Tax deductions are one valuable way to reduce your tax bill. They lower your taxes by the rate in your tax bracket. Thus, if you are in the 22 percent tax bracket, a $100 deduction will reduce your federal income taxes by $22. Tax credits are even more valuable. They lower your taxes dollar for dollar, so a $100 tax credit will shrink your tax bill by the full $100.

Common Tax Credits

Child Tax Credit. The 2021 American Rescue Plan included several provisions aimed at reducing child poverty. One change that could dramatically lower parents' tax bills is the increase in the Child Tax Credit from $2,000 to $3,600, for children younger than 6, and to $3,000, for children 6 through 17. You must claim the child on your tax return to earn the credit.

You can't take the full credit if you earn more than $75,000 (filing Single) or $112,500 (filing Head of Household). A tool on the IRS website (www.irs.gov) can help you estimate your Child Tax Credit.

Child and Dependent Care Tax Credit. You may be eligible for a tax credit if you pay for the care of a child under age 13, a disabled child or an elderly parent so you can work, actively seek employment or go to school full time. Payments to a day-care center, nanny or a babysitter (including grandparents) are eligible expenses. The American Rescue Plan significantly enhanced this credit as well, increasing the expenses that qualify for the credit to $8,000 for one qualifying child and $16,000 for two or more qualifying children—more than double the previous thresholds of $3,000 and $6,000, respectively. Also, the maximum percentage of eligible expenses that can be taken as a tax credit was increased from 35 percent to 50 percent. A single woman paying for day care for her twin four-year-olds and earning less than $125,000 could take a tax credit of $8,000 (50 percent of $16,000)—almost four times her credit under the old rules. And like the Child Tax Credit, the Child and Dependent Care Tax Credit is fully refundable: if your credit exceeds your tax bill, you'll get a check for the difference.

Note: As of this writing, enhancements to the Child Tax Credit and the Child and Dependent Care Tax Credit included in the American Rescue Plan apply to tax year 2021 only. However, there is a strong push to make both changes permanent.

Quick Tip: If you have one child and your income is over $125,000, you may save more by contributing to a Flexible Spending Account (FSA) through your employer rather than claiming the Child and Dependent Care Tax Credit. Contributions to an FSA for childcare (up to $10,500 in 2021) are excluded from federal, state, Social Security and Medicare taxes. Thus, if you contribute $200 to your FSA each week, your paycheck may only be reduced by $140 (depending on your tax bracket). When you submit your expense receipts, you are reimbursed up to the full amount you contributed to the FSA. You pocket the difference between the deduction from your paycheck ($140 in our example) and the amount you are reimbursed ($200).

American Opportunity and Lifetime Learning College Credits. If you or your dependent is enrolled at least half-time in a college degree program, you may be eligible for an American Opportunity Tax Credit (AOTC) of up to $2,500. The credit is available for the first four years of higher education. You get the tax credit if you claim the student, no matter who pays the tuition bills. Your income must be $80,000 or less to claim the full $2,500 credit (for single and head of household filers in 2021). If your income is between $80,000 and $90,000, you can claim a partial credit, and the credit disappears for incomes over $90,000.

Are you heading to graduate school or taking courses to improve your job skills? The Lifetime Learning Tax Credit provides a credit of 20 percent of up to $10,000 of tuition. The same income limits as the AOTC apply.

Earned Income Tax Credit. If you file as Single or as Head of Household and you earn less than $51,464 (in 2021), you may be eligible for the Earned Income Tax Credit. The 2021 American Rescue Plan increased the minimum credit from $543 to $1,502 for a single taxpayer with no children and up to $6,728 for a single person with three or more children. Individuals between 19 and 24 and age 65 and older became eligible, as of this writing, for the credit. To see if you qualify, read the instructions on the IRS website or consult a tax preparer.

HEALTH SAVINGS ACCOUNTS

A Health Savings Account (HSA) is a tax-advantaged savings account that can be used to pay for qualified medical expenses. You deduct contributions to an HSA from your taxable income (even if you don't itemize), and you aren't taxed on money you use for qualified out-of-pocket medical costs. This feature makes HSAs even more financially rewarding than Roth IRAs if used for out-of-pocket medical costs. If you withdraw money from an HSA, to splurge on a vacation, for instance, you'll owe ordinary income tax plus a 20 percent penalty on the amount you take out unless you are 65 or older.

To fund an HSA, you must enroll in a high-deductible health insurance plan—meaning your deductible is at least $1,400 a year for an individual or $2,800 for a family (defined as an individual and one other person). You can contribute to your HSA each year you participate in a high-deductible plan—up to $3,600 for an individual or $7,200 for a family in 2021—plus an additional $1,000 if you are 55 or older.

You can set up an HSA through your employer or on your own with a bank or other financial institution. Keep your HSA money in a low-risk investment such as a savings account if you plan to use the money for current medical expenses. If you plan to pay out-of-pocket medical expenses from another source, you could invest your contributions in a mutual fund within your HSA in order to let it grow tax-free. Unlike Flexible Savings Accounts, you keep HSA plans even if you change jobs or retire.

TAX-SMART WAYS OF SAVINGS

Most tax-advantaged retirement plans are doubly beneficial: they allow you to defer or postpone the amount you owe in taxes, and that money could be used to bolster the size of your retirement accounts.

More information about these retirement plans—including the benefits Roth IRAs provide—is contained in chapter 11.

Retirement plans come with built-in tax savings, but there are ways to pare your tax bill on nonretirement investments as well. For example, the interest earned on municipal bonds is free from federal taxes—as well as state taxes if you buy bonds issued by your resident state or city. You can buy individual bonds, but a less risky and more convenient method is to purchase shares of a municipal bond mutual fund or an exchange-traded fund (ETF).

You can defer paying taxes on profits earned in stock funds by investing in index mutual funds (that track a particular benchmark, such as the S&P 500) or ETFs. You will generally defer paying taxes on the profits until you sell shares. In contrast, actively managed funds, in which managers buy and sell stocks more frequently, often distribute profits or capital gains each year. You pay taxes on those distributions even if you invest the distributed gains right back into the fund and even if you didn't sell any shares.

Quick Tip: Distributions of capital gains from mutual funds are typically made at the end of the year. If you are unlucky enough to purchase shares of a mutual fund days before it distributes capital gains, you will pay tax on those gains even though you didn't own the fund long enough to earn a profit. Granted, when you sell the shares that were distributed and reinvested—sometime in the future—you'll get credit for the taxes you paid. But who wants a year-end tax surprise? Instead, avoid buying shares of an actively traded mutual fund during the last quarter of the year—or stick to index funds that rarely distribute gains.

TAX PENALTIES

The IRS will tack on a penalty to your taxes if you wait too long to pay. There are three ways to avoid an underpayment penalty:

1. Pay more than 90 percent of your tax bill for the current year by withholding taxes (from your paycheck, pension, IRA withdrawal or Social Security benefits) or by making quarterly estimated payments.

2. Withhold taxes or make quarterly estimated payments that total at least as much as your tax liability from the previous year (or 110 percent of that amount if you make more than $150,000).

3. Owe less than $1,000 when you file, as long as you have paid in the rest of your taxes through withholding or estimated payments. *Note:* Trying to avoid a penalty by making a big tax payment at the end of the year rarely works. The IRS expects you to pay four equal estimates, one each on April 15, June 15, September 15 and January 15, unless you can show the extra taxes are owed on income earned late in the year. Conversely, taxes paid through withholding (e.g., from a paycheck) can occur any time during the year. If you predict a tax shortfall, you may be able to change your withholding to cover the gap and avoid a penalty.

The IRS has a couple of handy tools on its website: a calculator to make sure your employer is withholding enough taxes (www.irs.gov/individuals/tax-withholding-estimator) and a worksheet on Form 1040-ES to figure your estimated taxes if you're self-employed (www.irs.gov/pub/irs-pdf/f1040es.pdf).

AND IF YOU CAN'T AFFORD YOUR TAX BILL?

If you don't have the funds to pay your tax bill, you have three options:

1. File your taxes on time (to avoid a late filing penalty), and pay as much as you can. Then pay the rest (plus any interest that has accumulated) as soon as you can.

2. Work out a payment installment plan with the IRS. Although you will still owe interest on the unpaid balance, arranging a monthly payment plan may relieve some stress.

3. Try to negotiate a compromise with the IRS—an agreement to pay less than the amount you owe based on your financial circumstances. You may wish to enlist the help of a CPA to negotiate with the IRS on your behalf.

11

PREPARING FOR THE RETIREMENT YOU WANT

How would you like to spend your "golden years"? Perhaps cruising on the Amazon or hiking in the Grand Tetons? What about volunteering in your community or taking courses at a local university? Or turning your passion for photography into a new career? You'll likely have plenty of time to work through your wish list, since retirement can last 30 years or longer.

When you have enough savings and investments—along with your Social Security and any pension income—you can cut the cord to your monthly paycheck and live the life you wish.

But how much is "enough"? Is there some marker, some defined sum of money guaranteed to last you through retirement? Can you amass the money you'll need at your current savings rate? The answers to these two questions are no and yes. Contrary to what some experts believe, there is no one amount of money that assures you a comfortable, wish-fulfilling retirement. But by creating a solid plan for your future, you better your odds of a rewarding life ahead. And the earlier you start planning and saving for retirement, the more likely you'll fulfill your retirement dreams.

HOW MUCH DO YOU NEED?

To many experts, retirees need 75 percent to 80 percent of their pre-retirement income to cover their costs. But that rough estimate varies with lifestyle, housing and health care costs, among other expenses.

How do you know how much money you'll need in retirement? That calculation involves several easy steps that compare your expected funds in retirement to your desired lifestyle.

It starts by reviewing your current expenses. If you are within five years of retirement, create a budget for your nonworking years. Tally how much you spend now on such items as mortgage or rent, groceries, medical insurance and the like. Add higher future expenses such as travel. Then subtract costs that will no longer apply when you are not working. If retirement is more than five years off, simply use current monthly expenses as a guide to future costs.

After you've estimated your retirement spending, compute how to pay for it. Figure out whether your current savings rate will be enough to fund your retirement when added to Social Security and other income, such as a pension. For help with that computation, use an online tool, such as the Schwab Retirement Savings Calculator at www.schwab.com (search for "retirement calculator"). After you answer a few basic questions, these calculators will reveal how close you are to meeting your financial goals.

But what if the calculator has bad news? What if your savings and future income won't cover your retirement costs, dashing your plans? That's possible, since many single women struggle to save on a low salary. So recalibrate: trim your plans for future spending or boost your current savings rate—or do both. Some other options to help you afford your retirement include:

- Working longer—at least until age 70, when you can claim your maximum Social Security benefit.
- Working after you retire. Even a part-time job can cover some of your bills and preserve your savings. Look for work that uses the skills you have honed during your career or that matches your interests. For example, if you retired as an accountant, consider keeping books for a small business or local nonprofit. Or if you

love the theater, look for work at a local performing arts center. If you retire before age 65, which is when you can apply for Medicare, seek a job that provides health insurance.

- Paring your plans for retirement. Review your retirement spending plan and highlight the categories that could be adjusted. A trip every other year or travel to closer destinations may be more affordable. "Test drive" your plan by living on your retirement budget while you are still working.

- Downsizing your home—even before you retire. Lowering your monthly payment, property taxes and maintenance can free up money for retirement spending. A recent study by the Employee Benefit Research Institute (EBRI) and J.P. Morgan concluded that spending less on housing and cars freed up money for savings more successfully than cutting back on so-called discretionary expenses such as eating out.[1] It's just too easy to slip back into old habits.

- Investing more heavily in stocks rather than in bonds, to boost your long-term investment returns. As described in chapter 7, the scanty earnings on CDs and savings accounts will replace only a tiny portion of the money you withdraw for spending. The higher average return you can earn on a balanced group of investments is more likely to extend the life of your savings.

- Steadily increasing your savings rate. Aim to put away 15 percent of your income each year while you're working. To get there, bump up contributions to your retirement plan each time you get a raise and contribute at least some of your bonus.

- Adding your accumulated sick and vacation pay to your retirement account. If you are allowed to cash in a portion of your unused vacation days each year, put that money into an IRA or savings account. In addition, when you leave your employer, you may get a lump sum to cover unused sick and vacation days. If so, ask if that money can be added to your 401(k) or other retirement plan. Besides enhancing savings, this money will grow tax-deferred.

WHERE TO SAVE

How do you wade through the available array of plans and accounts to decide where to invest your retirement savings? You may be eligible to contribute to more than one type of account, and the rules differ among plans. Which one you choose depends on where you work, how much you earn, your tax bracket and how disciplined a saver you are. A table near the end of this chapter will help you pinpoint the best plan for your situation.

To boost your savings, choose a plan that offers a tax benefit, either when you invest or when you withdraw your money. Traditional IRAs and company plans such as 401(k) and 403(b) accounts combine two tax breaks: your contributions are generally deducted from your taxable income, and the earnings on your investments grow tax-deferred. You pay taxes on both the contributions and earnings when you withdraw money from the plan. Roth IRAs and Roth versions of employer plans work differently. You contribute with after-tax money—no tax break there—but as long as you follow the rules, your withdrawals will be tax-free.

Employer Plans

The most common employer-sponsored plan is the 401(k) plan, named after a section of the IRS code. These plans were designed to supplement traditional pension plans—a way for workers to stash away their own money to bolster their retirement security. Since over time, companies eliminated or froze their pensions, 401(k) plans have become the sole retirement savings for most workers. This has shifted the burden of savings from employers to their workers.

Saving in a 401(k) plan is fairly straightforward. Sign up with your human resources or payroll department, figure out how much you can afford to contribute from each paycheck and choose your investments from a list offered by the plan. In an effort to encourage saving, some employers enroll new employees automatically in the company retirement plan.

When you participate, your employer subtracts your contribution before you get your paycheck. That guarantees you fund your retirement account before spending the money elsewhere. And because the money is pulled from your pay "pre-tax," your contributions go further. A $100 deposit in your 401(k) plan will only reduce your paycheck by about $80 because you save federal and state income taxes on the contribution.

Many employers add money to your 401(k) plan by matching your contributions. A typical match is 100 percent of the money you put in, up to 3 percent of your salary. If possible, contribute at least enough to get the full employer match. Generally, you can keep the matching funds after you work for your employer a set period, typically three to five years. Under such an arrangement, called vesting, a portion of the match is yours each year until the full amount vests. At that time, you own the entire account even if you leave the company.

If you resign or retire, you can roll over your 401(k) account into your own IRA or your new employer's 401(k) plan. If your balance is at least $5,000, you also have the option of leaving the money in your former employer's plan.

The maximum you can contribute to a 401(k) plan is $19,500 in 2021 ($26,000 if you are 50 or older) or 100 percent of your salary, whichever is less. The Summary Plan Description, which employers must provide, contains all the rules for your plan.

A similar type of retirement plan, called a 403(b) plan or Tax-Sheltered Annuity (TSA), is typically offered by public schools or nonprofit organizations, such as some hospitals. The rules are generally the same as those governing 401(k) plans, except a "catch-up" provision may allow you to contribute more to your 403(b) plan as you get close to retirement. And unlike 401(k) plans, where you select your investments from one list, the 403(b) often comes with an array of plan providers.

Since you choose the provider, scrutinize your options carefully. And be sure to ask about fees, which can eat into your bottom line. For example, the fees of most 403(b) plans offered by insurance companies are often 2 percent higher than those charged by mutual fund companies such as Vanguard. That extra 2 percent adds up. As shown in figure 11.1, if you invest $200 a month over 20 years in a high-cost 403(b) plan that deducts 2.5 percent a year for fees, you will end up with over $15,000 less in your account than if you invested the same amount in a low-cost plan charging 0.5 percent a year.

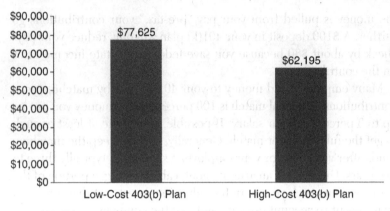

Note: Balances after 20 years of investing $200 per month in a mutual fund earning 5% per year
Low-cost plan expenses =0.5%; high-cost plan expenses =2.5%

**Figure 11.1.   Plan Expenses Make a Difference: Account Balances in
Low-Cost vs. High-Cost 403(b) Plan.** *Source:* Authors.

If you're a government employee, you may have the opportunity
to contribute to a 457 plan, also called a deferred compensation plan.
The rules are very similar to those of 401(k) and 403(b) plans, with
two notable exceptions. If you are near retirement and did not contribute the maximum amount in earlier years, you may be able to add
as much as $39,000 in one year. And withdrawals prior to age 59½ are
not subject to a 10 percent penalty, although you will still pay ordinary
income tax on the amount you take out.

Contributing to an employer plan is convenient but be sure to avoid
mistakes. The major "don'ts" to bear in mind include:

- Don't borrow. Although many plans allow you to borrow as much
  as 50 percent of your vested balance up to $50,000 and repay the
  loan over five years or more, it's unwise to do so. You could lose
  money in two ways: the money you withdraw will no longer be
  invested, risking a loss of earnings on the sum you withdrew. And
  if you leave the company, the loan may be reclassified as a taxable distribution. You could owe regular federal and state income
  taxes on the unpaid balance and an additional 10 percent penalty
  if you are younger than 59½.

- Don't forfeit the match. Contribute at least enough to earn the full amount the employer will put into your account.
- Don't invest too conservatively. The money you put into a 401(k) plan will stay there (or in a rollover IRA) until you retire—or longer. You will have time to wait out the ups and downs of the stock market, so invest at least 50 percent in stock mutual funds.
- Don't ignore opportunities to increase your contributions. Most years, the IRS bumps up the contribution limits; follow suit and increase the amount you put into the plan.
- Don't cash in your 401(k) account when you leave an employer. Keep your money in the plan or roll it over to an IRA or your new employer's plan. If you cash in your account, you'll pay taxes, and perhaps a penalty, which means an instant loss of 20 percent to 40 percent of your balance.

If you work for a small firm or you are self-employed, you may prefer a SIMPLE-IRA or SEP-IRA (Simplified Employee Pension IRA). With the SIMPLE-IRA, the tax advantages mirror those of 401(k) and other plans, but the contribution limit is lower: $13,500 in 2021 ($16,500 if you are 50 or older). However, your contributions and employer match vest immediately. And the rules for withdrawing money are unique to SIMPLE-IRAs: if you are younger than 59½ and withdraw money within the first two years of joining the plan, you must pay income taxes plus a 25 percent penalty on money you withdraw.

In contrast, SEP-IRAs are particularly attractive if you own a small business. With this plan, you are eligible to contribute 20 percent of your net income (or profits), up to $58,000 (in 2021). Thus, if you rake in $100,000 in profits, you can deduct fully $20,000 from your taxable income that year. You can create a SEP-IRA as late as April 15 of the following year—or October 15 if you file an extension on your personal income tax return. SEP-IRAs work best if you own your own business and have no employees. If you have employees, it can get expensive: you must contribute the same percentage of their salary as you get.

IRAs

If you don't have access to an employer's retirement plan or if you prefer your own plan, consider opening an IRA. There are two flavors: traditional and Roth. If you have earned income (from a job or self-employment), you can contribute up to $6,000 in 2021 ($7,000 if you are 50 or older) or the amount you earn that year—whichever amount is lower—to a traditional IRA. If you are not covered by a retirement plan at work, deduct your IRA contribution from your taxable income to get the tax benefit. As mentioned in chapter 10, your investments grow tax-deferred until you withdraw the money. If you are 59½ or older, you'll pay income taxes on the amount withdrawn. But if you are younger than 59½, you'll pay a 10 percent penalty on top of the income taxes. The penalty is meant to discourage you from withdrawing money before retirement.

If you're in a retirement plan at work, you have different rules: you can deduct your full IRA contribution each year from taxable income if your adjusted gross income is less than $66,000 (filing as a single person, in 2021). Between $66,000 and $76,000 of income, you can deduct part of your IRA contribution; but if your income exceeds $76,000, you lose the deduction. Thus, if you do earn more than $76,000, it's usually not worth contributing to a traditional IRA.

The Roth IRA is a newer model: available since 1997, it has become the option of choice for many savers. Contribution limits are the same as those of traditional IRAs—the lesser of your earned income or $6,000 ($7,000 if 50 or older). If you are not working, you can't contribute to either a traditional or Roth IRA. If you file Single or Head of Household, you can contribute to a Roth IRA if your adjusted gross income is lower than $125,000 (in 2021). If your income falls between $125,000 and $140,000, you can contribute a prorated amount, but if your income exceeds $140,000, you can't add money to a Roth IRA.

You pay taxes on contributions to a Roth IRA the year you make them. Withdrawals are tax-free if you're 59½ or older and you've made your first Roth contribution at least five years earlier. And you may take out your original contributions any time tax- and penalty-free. Thus a Roth IRA can serve a dual purpose: it's a way to save for your future while also funding emergencies that may occur sooner.

If you are eligible to contribute to both a traditional and a Roth IRA, you can add money to both accounts as long as the total does not exceed $6,000 (or $7,000) a year. You can double-dip by contributing to your 401(k), 403(b) or 457 plan via your paycheck and contributing to an IRA on your own, if your income is within the specified limits. What if you're shut out from using Roth IRAs because of your high income? If your employer offers a Roth option in a 401(k), 403(b) or 457 plan, you can designate that option for all or part of your contributions. Although you'll get no up-front tax deduction, your investment earnings will grow tax-free. When you leave the company, you can roll the Roth portion of your account into a Roth IRA, while the rest of your retirement assets go into a traditional IRA.

Newer Options

The good news for those without a retirement plan at work: as of August 31, 2020, in 12 states and 1 city, you automatically join your state-sponsored savings program, according to the Georgetown University Center for Retirement Initiatives.[2] Under these plans, employees contribute part of their paycheck—up to $6,000 per year ($7,000 if over age 50)—to a traditional or Roth IRA and can opt out at any time. And there's no cost to employers.

Among other proposed changes: if you're a low-income taxpayer, the tax deduction on your retirement savings would be converted to a tax credit, which is a more generous benefit; and, anyone who quits work to care for a family member could contribute to a retirement account even without earning a paycheck.

Which Way to Save?

Start by identifying your options. Then decide whether you prefer an up-front tax break (from a traditional IRA or employer plan) or tax-free withdrawals in retirement (from a Roth IRA or the Roth version of an employer plan). If you expect your tax bracket—or tax rates, in general—will increase by the time you retire, you'll likely prefer the Roth option. Or hedge your bet: split your contributions between Roth and traditional accounts.

Table 11.1. Tax-Advantaged Options for Saving for Retirement

	Maximum Contribution	Contributions Tax Deductible?	Withdrawals Taxable?	Due Date to Contribute	Advantages
401(k) Plan	$19,500 ($26,000 if 50 or older)	Yes	Yes	December 31	Convenient; up-front tax break; employer may match
Roth 401(k) Plan	Same	No	No, if over 59½ and first contribution made at least 5 years ago	December 31	Convenient; contributions grow tax-free; employer may match
403(b) Plan	Same	Yes	Yes	December 31	Convenient; up-front tax break
Roth 403(b) Plan	Same	No	Same as Roth 401(k)	December 31	Convenient; money grows tax-free
457 Plan	Same	Yes	Yes	December 31	Convenient; up-front tax break
Roth 457 Plan	Same	No	Same as Roth 401(k)	December 31	Convenient; money grows tax-free
SEP-IRA	20% of profits up to $58,000	Yes	Yes	April 15 of next year (October 15 if you extend)	Easy to set up; good option for solo business
SIMPLE-IRA	$13,500 ($16,500 if 50 or older)	Yes	Yes	December 31	Easy to set up; good option for small business with employees
Traditional IRA	$6,000 ($7,000 if 50 or older)	Yes; if covered by another plan, deductibility may be limited	Yes	April 15 of next year	May be tax deductible; easy to open an account
Roth IRA	$6,000 ($7,000 if 50 or older)	No	No, if over 59½ and first contribution made at least 5 years ago	April 15 of next year	Grows tax-free; easy to open an account

Note: These rules were in effect as of January 2021.

If you own a small business, consider opening a SEP-IRA account (if you work solo) or a SIMPLE-IRA (if you have employees). If you are trying to rev up savings, contribute to both a 401(k) and an IRA. Table 11.1 summarizes your choices.

SPECIAL CASES

Retirement plans are often split during a divorce. A Qualified Domestic Relations Order (QDRO) is drawn up by an attorney to stipulate that all or part of a pension is to be paid to a former spouse. If you are the recipient, roll the lump sum into your own IRA or take monthly payments from a pension when you retire. However, if you are splitting an IRA due to divorce, avoid taxes by putting your share in your own IRA. Be sure to use a trustee-to-trustee transfer.

If you are a widow who inherits a 401(k) or other employer retirement plan or an IRA from your late spouse, you have choices:

• You can keep the money in the employer plan or roll it into an Inherited IRA that you create. Both options allow you to delay taking money until your spouse would have turned 72, under current rules. You must withdraw a larger amount each year than if you had owned the retirement account all along, but you will not pay a 10 percent penalty on withdrawals—even if you are younger than 59½. Thus, if you are a young widow and need to tap your deceased spouse's retirement accounts, keep the money in the employer's plan or roll it into an Inherited IRA.
• You may roll over a spouse's retirement plan or IRA into your own IRA. With this method, you start withdrawing money when you turn 72. This may work best if you are older than 59½ and will not be penalized for your withdrawals.

PUTTING IT ALL TOGETHER

Jenna, the 30-year-old woman whose story is told in chapter 6, and Barbara, an artist who was divorced several years ago, are at different stages in their retirement planning. How have they fared?

Jenna knows the $90 per paycheck she contributes to her employer's 457 retirement plan will likely not cover her retirement needs. However, she has two options for making retirement ends meet. If she completes at least five years of state or local government employment, she will receive a government annuity at age 67. In addition, she could shift the extra $100 a month she is paying on her mortgage into her 457 plan, which would save her $20 a month of income tax. She could put that $20 into the 457 plan, bringing the total new contribution to $120 a month. If Jenna averages a 5 percent return on her 457 plan investments, that extra $120 a month will total $154,000 when she retires decades from now—thanks to the benefit of compounding interest.

Barbara, a divorcée, was older than Jenna when she started saving on her own. That left her fewer years to amass the retirement assets she would eventually need. However, she made a smart decision: right after her divorce, she invested almost 30 percent of her alimony even though it was her only income. By the time Barbara's alimony stopped ten years later, her investments had quadrupled in value.

And, in retirement, she was set: Barbara had ample savings along with the Social Security benefits she received as a divorcée.

(12)

MAXIMIZING YOUR SOCIAL SECURITY BENEFIT

You imagine retiring comfortably down the road—and on your schedule. Perhaps that time will come at age 65 or even sooner. But whatever the retirement date, you expect to be ready, or so you think now.

But will you be financially set?

One crucial determinant could be the size of your check from the Social Security Administration. Once you're no longer employed, this monthly benefit, which you contributed to with your payroll deductions during working years, may be your only ongoing guaranteed retirement income. Thus you need to maximize this benefit, since you may live a long time in retirement.

Unfortunately, understanding the Social Security system isn't easy. Replete with clauses and if-then provisions, it may seem as complex as black hole theory. But you have to be paying heed: if you err, such as claiming Social Security too early for your long-term needs, you could lose money you'll need—and at a time when you can no longer work.

According to the Social Security Administration (SSA), the average earner's Social Security retirement benefit replaces about 40 percent of previous salary.[1] Although pensions and savings are supposed to fill in the rest of retirees' financial needs, pensions have become scarce, and savings may be limited, especially for those who've lived on one income. In fact, almost half of unmarried female retirees rely on Social Security for 90 percent or more of their retirement income.[2]

Thus, you have to know the best time to file for this benefit and, if previously married, the special rules for widows and divorcées.

BACKGROUND

When President Franklin Roosevelt signed the Social Security Act on August 14, 1935, it marked a sea change in the lives of older adults. In the 1930s, about half of seniors in the United States lived in poverty.[3] Social Security threw the elderly a lifeline, providing them with a way out of poverty, and enabled seniors to retire with fewer fears of financial ruin. In the ensuing years, Social Security expanded to include benefits for spouses, minor children and the disabled. In 1965, the Medicare program was created, providing health insurance for retired individuals 65 and older.

Social Security continues to be highly popular and successful. In 2018, its benefits lifted 8.7 million women out of poverty. Currently, about 11 percent of older women live below the poverty line but, without Social Security, about 41 percent of them would be impoverished, according to a study by the Center on Budget and Policy Priorities.[4]

The first person to receive monthly Social Security benefits was Ida May Fuller, a legal secretary from Vermont. Over her working life, she paid a total of $24.75 into the Social Security system but collected $22,888.92 in benefits by the time she died at age 100.[5]

Today, a woman earning an average salary who retired at age 65 in 2020, can expect, over her lifetime, to receive $589,000 in combined benefits—$332,000 in Social Security retirement payments and $257,000 in Medicare insurance—according to the Urban Institute.[6]

But here's the rising concern: the Social Security system could go broke. As designed, contributions from current workers fund the benefits for retirees. Any excess goes into a trust fund. In 1950, 16.5 workers paid into the program for every retired worker drawing benefits. As our population aged, that ratio has dwindled and, in 2020, only

2.8 workers contributed to Social Security for every person (retired or disabled) who received benefits.[7] By 2034, the Social Security Administration estimates the trust fund will be exhausted. Then, payroll taxes will only cover 76 percent of benefits.[8]

But don't be alarmed, especially if you are in or near retirement: it is unlikely the amount of your Social Security will be cut. Elected officials have consistently backed this system that is so crucial to seniors. Over the years, Congress avoided reducing Social Security benefits by raising the full retirement age and increasing payroll contributions. Or Congress could simply write a check to cover any Social Security shortfall, as it did to fund Medicaid expansion.

THE BASICS

You can qualify for Social Security benefits based on your own work record or on a former or deceased spouse's earnings. As of this writing, to qualify for benefits under your own work history, you need to accumulate at least 40 credits. You get a credit for every $1,470 you earn from a job or self-employment income (in 2021)—up to 4 credits per year. Thus, it takes at least 10 years to get the 40 credits needed to qualify for benefits. It gets more complicated from here: even if you earn more than $5,880 in a year, you cannot get more than 4 credits a year. But once you gain your 40 credits, your earnings—anything above $5,880—will boost your eventual Social Security benefits.

If you were previously married, you may receive benefits based on your former or deceased spouse's work history (as described below). Generally, you will receive the larger of your benefit or the benefit based on your spouse's record, although you may be able to maximize your income by receiving one benefit first and switching to the other later.

If you qualify for benefits based on your own earnings, Social Security will use 35 years of work history to calculate your benefit. If you worked longer than 35 years, Social Security counts only the 35 years of your highest wages.

If you did not work 35 years, you will have some zeroes in your work history, reducing your benefit. But by working part-time you can fill in some of the blank years and boost your Social Security income.

Social Security uses a complicated formula to calculate your monthly benefit. Because it is designed to be social insurance—and not a conventional pension—lower-paid workers receive a higher percentage of their wages when they draw benefits. Higher-paid workers receive a larger monthly check but a smaller percentage of their salary. Here's an example based on the Quick Calculator on the Social Security Administration website (www.ssa.gov): a woman who is 62 in 2020 and earns an average of $3,000 a month will receive $1,456 at age 66 and 10 months (her full retirement age, described below) or almost half of her salary. If the same person earned $8,000 a month on average, her benefit would be higher—$2,797 a month—but Social Security would only replace about a third of her salary. It makes sense: if you earn more, you should be able to put more aside for retirement and depend less on Social Security.

BENEFITS FOR OTHER FAMILY MEMBERS

But Social Security isn't just for you. Over 3 million children a year receive benefits from it, keeping 1.2 million children out of poverty, according to the Center on Budget and Policy Priorities.[9]

Consider: if you are collecting Social Security retirement or disability benefits and caring for an unmarried child, your child may be eligible for a benefit equal to 50 percent of what you are receiving. To be eligible, your child must be younger than 18, or younger than 19 if a full-time elementary or high school student. If disabled before age 22, a child is eligible for benefits past age 18.

CHOOSING YOUR DATE

The surest way to boost your Social Security benefit is to delay claiming it. Three key ages to consider are:

Age 62. The earliest you can receive Social Security benefits is age 62 (although widows can start as early as age 60). At first glance, earlier sounds better. According to a study by Nationwide Retirement Institute, 74 percent of women surveyed took their Social Security benefits early. Here's the rub: your check will be cut by 25 percent to 30 percent for the rest of your life if you take benefits at age 62 (considered "early retirement age") compared to waiting until your full retirement age (between 66 and 67). As the Nationwide study concludes, by settling for a smaller check at age 62, you are effectively "locking in a lifetime of lower income."[10]

If you are still working and take Social Security before your full retirement age, you're probably erring on two fronts. While you're working, you reduce your benefit $1 for every $2 you earn above the annual limit ($18,960 in 2021). And like anyone who takes Social Security early, you are getting a lower benefit than you'd get at full retirement age. Thus the best solution: wait until at least your full retirement age to collect.

Full Retirement Age. You are eligible for full, unreduced Social Security benefits at your full retirement age. If you were born between 1943 and 1954, your full retirement age is 66; it increases gradually and tops out at age 67 for those born in 1960 or later, under current rules. You can find your exact full retirement age on the Social Security website (www.ssa.gov).

If you continue working past your full retirement age, your monthly benefit will be bumped up twice each year—once for the annual cost-of-living increase and once to reflect your continuing contributions to Social Security.

Age 70. If you plan to collect benefits based on your own work history, wait until age 70 if at all possible. This will give you the maximum possible benefit, since Social Security benefits increase 8 percent annually between full retirement age and 70. This gives you more money than you'd make on CDs or money market accounts, which haven't paid 8 percent for 30 years.

Waiting beyond age 70 for Social Security is useless. If your 70th birthday slips by and you forget to apply for benefits, you can receive up to 6 months of retroactive benefits—but your monthly amount will be the same as at age 70.

So what is the ideal age to start benefits? Not surprisingly, it depends on a range of personal and financial circumstances, and the math can be tricky. The following stories show how three women evaluated their choices and figured out the best strategy for their retirement.

Alice: Never Married

Take the hypothetical case of Alice, who retired in 2020 when she was 60. Because she never married, her Social Security benefit will be based on her own work history. At age 62, she can file for early Social Security payments of $1,100 per month. But if Alice waits until her full retirement age of 67, her monthly Social Security check will be about $1,560. If she waits until she's 70, she'll get $1,937 a month, which is a whopping 76 percent higher than her $1,100 a month benefit at age 62. Of course, Alice will need other sources of income—from savings or part-time jobs—to cover her expenses between age 62 and when she starts drawing benefits. But the larger Social Security check can ease her biggest fear in retirement—running out of money in old age.

Carmen: Divorced

Consider the hypothetical case of Carmen, a 60-year-old divorcée who retired in 2020. Like many divorced or widowed people, she's likely to be daunted by Social Security and its many options for ex-spouses.

Over the years, Carmen has worked periodically as a part-time sales clerk. At her full retirement age of 67, she will be entitled to a $600-a-month Social Security benefit. She is also eligible to receive benefits based on her former husband's work record because they were married 20 years before they divorced (10 years is the minimum to qualify). Her ex-husband won't lose his $2,000 monthly benefit at age 67.

If Carmen also waits until age 67 to apply for Social Security, she will automatically receive half of her ex-husband's benefit, which gives her $1,000. That's larger than the $600 she would get from her own benefit.

Would Carmen receive more than $1,000 a month if she waited until age 70? No. Only benefits based on one's own work record increase in value between full retirement age and age 70. Thus, Carmen's spousal benefit would not increase by waiting to collect past age 67.

But if Carmen remarries? She forfeits the $1,000 a month based on her ex-husband's record. Instead she will receive the larger of her benefit or half of her new husband's benefit. Alternatively, if Carmen remains single and her ex-husband dies, when she files, she will get the more generous widow's benefit: 100 percent of what her ex-spouse received, if she is 67 or older, or between 71 percent and 99 percent if she is between 60 and 67.

Cynthia: Widowed

Cynthia became a widow in 2019. After her husband died, she retired in 2020 at age 60. She had been employed most of her adult life and qualifies for $1,400 a month of Social Security at age 67, based on her own work record. Her husband had worked longer and earned a higher salary, entitling him to a higher Social Security benefit of $2,000 a month at full retirement age.

If Cynthia applies for a widow's benefit at 67, she will collect 100 percent of her husband's $2,000 monthly entitlement. If she applies now, at age 60 (the earliest date possible for a widow to receive benefits), she'll get only $1,430 a month (71.5 percent of her husband's $2,000).

But Cynthia has better, albeit more complex, options. Let's say she applied for a widow's benefit at age 60 and started collecting $1,430 a month. Then, at age 70, she can switch to a benefit based on her own work record, increasing her monthly Social Security check to $1,736. By collecting a widow's benefit starting at age 60 and switching to her own benefit at 70, she boosts her lifetime Social Security income by $75,000.

Cynthia's other option is her best bet: starting at age 62, she collects $986 a month based on her own work record. Then, at age 67, she switches to her widow's benefit, which is $2,000 a month—the amount her ex-spouse was collecting. That's more than the $1,736 top amount she would have collected in the example above. (*Note:* If her former spouse had not yet filed for benefits, Cynthia would collect the amount her ex was eligible to receive.)

But your situation may differ. If you and your deceased spouse had comparable work histories and were entitled to similar Social Security benefits, you'd maximize your Social Security by starting your widow's benefit when eligible and switching to your own benefit at age 70.

Amid all this complexity, you have to wonder how people get every penny they deserve. Start by creating your own Social Security account at www.ssa.gov/myaccount. Among its features, it allows you to review your work history and project your future benefits. When you are a few years away from retirement age, meet with a representative at your local Social Security office to evaluate your options.

OTHER CONSIDERATIONS

Taxes

The federal government taxes Social Security benefits on a sliding scale based on your other income. If you are single, it works this way: if half of your Social Security benefits plus your other income including non-taxed items (such as municipal bond interest) total between $25,000 and $34,000, you'll pay taxes on your Social Security benefits at your regular income tax rate. But that's only on up to 50 percent of these benefits. At higher incomes, you'll be taxed on up to 85 percent of your benefits.

To owe less at tax time, ask the Social Security Administration to withhold federal taxes on your benefits by filing form W-4V (available at www.ssa.gov). But you may still owe state income tax on your benefits. Happily, 37 states plus the District of Columbia do not tax Social Security benefits.

Changing Your Mind

What if you applied for benefits early and later regretted it? If you have not yet reached your full retirement age, you can withdraw your application within 12 months of applying and repay all the benefits you received. Later you can reapply to get a higher benefit. You can only do this once. If you are between your full retirement age and 70, you can ask Social Security to suspend your benefits. They resume automatically when you turn 70 unless you restart them sooner.

Missing Earnings

It's a good idea to check your Social Security statement online every few years to make sure all the information is correct and your annual wages have been properly reported. If earnings are missing, gather any evidence such as your W-2 or a paystub and contact Social Security to ensure you get your full benefits.

Windfall and Offset Rules

If you taught in a public school or university or worked in local government, you may not have contributed to Social Security. Instead, you may have paid into a government pension plan. If so, you are entitled to your full pension, but according to the Windfall Elimination and Government Pension Offset rules, your Social Security benefits may be reduced. (Pensions from private companies do not reduce Social Security benefits.)

The Windfall Elimination rule applies to widows and divorced people. If you receive a government pension and are entitled to Social Security benefits as a widow or ex-spouse, the government subtracts two-thirds of your pension from your Social Security check. For example, if your teacher's pension is $1,200 per month and you are a widow, you'll lose $800 of your Social Security benefits.

For anyone entitled to a government pension who also contributed to Social Security, the Government Pension Offset provision may reduce Social Security benefits based on your own work history. It gets very complicated. Generally, if you contributed to Social Security for 30 years, you will receive your pension and full Social Security benefits. But if you contributed to Social Security for fewer than 30 years, you will lose part of your Social Security benefits based on a sliding scale. Calculators on the Social Security website (www.ssa.gov) can help you figure out the amount your benefits will be reduced, or a representative at your local Social Security office can assist you.

DISABILITY BENEFITS

If your medical condition is likely to last more than a year or cause your death, you can apply for Social Security Disability Insurance (SSDI). You must have earned at least 20 credits in the 10 years prior to your disability, if you are 31 or older. If you are younger, different rules apply.

The monthly payment is far from generous. According to the Social Security Administration, in 2019 the average benefit paid to disabled workers was $1,234 a month: "barely enough to keep a beneficiary above the 2018 poverty level."[11]

Moreover, qualifying for SSDI is difficult. By some estimates, as many as 70 percent of first-time applications are denied. According to the Social Security Administration, 35 percent of disability applications received in 2020 were approved.[12]

Instead of relying solely on SSDI, consider buying a disability policy with a private insurance company, or obtain it at work if it's offered. Check your policy: if you're getting both SSDI and benefits from a private plan, your payout from a private plan may be reduced if both benefits exceed 80 percent of your earnings when working.

MEDICARE

You are eligible for Medicare insurance at age 65, no matter when you start collecting Social Security retirement benefits. If you are receiving Social Security disability benefits, you are eligible for Medicare after a 24-month waiting period.

If you apply for Medicare during your "enrollment period"—up to three months before your 65th birthday and three months afterward—you will pay the standard premium (plus any income-related adjustment, explained below). Don't miss that enrollment window. Your premium will be 10 percent higher for the rest of your life for every 12-month period you were eligible for Medicare and did not apply. You are exempt from that higher premium if you are 65 or older and are covered by group health insurance. But be sure to sign up for Medicare as soon as that coverage ends. If you are on a COBRA plan from a previous employer, you must apply for Medicare when you turn 65 to avoid a penalty.

Figuring out Medicare is like learning the alphabet. Since it was signed into law in 1965, Medicare has expanded to include Parts A, B, D and C. Medicare Part C is now known as Medicare Advantage.

Medicare Part A covers hospital costs and, in some cases, up to 100 days of skilled nursing care. Part A is free if you paid into Medicare for at least 40 quarters. Otherwise, you can purchase Part A for between $259 and $471 a month (in 2021).

Medicare Part B covers doctor bills and outpatient care. The premium is $148.50 per month (in 2021) if you are single and your income is under $87,000. You'll pay more if your income is higher. To check Medicare premiums at different income levels, go to www .medicare.gov and search for "IRMAA," the acronym for the rule governing premiums. Since your Medicare premium is calculated each year, a one-year jump in income will boost your premiums only for a year.

The federal government runs Medicare Parts A and B, known as "traditional Medicare." Private insurance companies offer Medicare Advantage plans, which take the place of Parts A and B (and sometimes Part D). Although the premium is the same as traditional Medicare's is, you may receive additional benefits from Advantage plans, such as prescription drug coverage and vision and dental insurance. It sounds like a good deal, and it may be the right choice for you, but make sure you read the fine print. One risk: Advantage plans generally restrict coverage to a list of doctors and hospitals, and the list may not include your preferred practitioners.

If you choose Medicare Parts A and B, you can add Part D to cover prescription drugs. By entering your address and the prescriptions you currently take on www.medicare.gov, you can get a list of companies available in your area and the monthly premium you would pay for adding Part D.

The final piece of the Medicare puzzle is the Medicare supplement called "Medigap." This is private insurance that pays many expenses not covered by traditional Medicare. According to America's Health Insurance Plans (AHIP), about a third of recipients of traditional Medicare buy this extra insurance.[13] Medigap plans are categorized as A through L, depending on the benefits offered. All plans with the same letter offer essentially the same coverage, simplifying the shopping process. If you purchase a Medigap plan within six months of turning 65, you cannot be turned down or charged more for preexisting medical conditions.

FINAL THOUGHTS

Deciding when to apply for Social Security benefits is an important—but often daunting—task. The process is more manageable if you break it down into steps:

1. Check your Social Security statement to make sure all your earnings are accurately reported. You can download a statement if you set up a "*my* Social Security" account on the Social Security website (www.ssa.gov).
2. Study your options. The Social Security Administration publishes helpful booklets (available on their website), including several focused on women's choices.
3. Try out some scenarios. The Retirement Estimator and the Life Expectancy Calculator are two helpful tools available on the website.
4. Talk to a professional. Make an appointment with your local Social Security office to review your options. Consider working with a financial planner who is knowledgeable about Social Security to help you devise a strategy. For more information about hiring a planner, see chapter 7.

13

MAKING YOUR MONEY LAST

What will you do if your money runs out in old age?

Evidently, that fear—of going broke when you can no longer work—is rampant among women, even among high earners. Consider these sobering statistics: in a study by Allianz Insurance, 57 percent of women said that the prospect of running out of money in retirement kept them awake at night. In addition, 27 percent of women earning $200,000 a year or more worried about ending up a bag lady—homeless and dragging possessions in a shopping bag.[1]

Happily, such a grim fate doesn't have to be yours. By planning ahead, with specific strategies for managing your income and safely tapping your savings, you can feel comfortable that you won't outlast your money, even through a long retirement.

Of course, you're dealing with many unknowns: you can't say exactly how much your savings and other assets will tally at retirement. And you can't predict what emergencies will arise in old age. But you can and should create a flexible retirement budget, one that matches your expected retirement resources with your estimated spending in retirement.

The riskiest part involves using your savings. In retirement, those crucial funds cover the gap between your guaranteed income, such as Social Security, and your costs, including any emergencies. The dilemma: taking out too much may deplete your savings, but withdrawing too little could limit your lifestyle.

How do you determine how much to withdraw if you don't know how long you'll live—or how healthy you'll be? There's no crystal ball. That means you need to adopt a withdrawal strategy, one based solidly on investment and longevity data.

DETERMINING HOW MUCH TO WITHDRAW

A starting point is the 4-percent rule, developed by financial advisor William Bengen in 1994.[2] Simply put, your investments are likely to last 30 years if you withdraw 4 percent of the total during your first year in retirement and adjust that amount for inflation in subsequent years. Let's say you retire with $300,000 in savings and investments. You can cash in $12,000 (4 percent of $300,000) the first year you tap your portfolio. If inflation averages 2 percent, the next year you can withdraw $12,000 plus 2 percent to offset inflation for a total of $12,240 ($12,000 times 1.02). If you would rather not look up the inflation rate each year, you can assume inflation will average 2 percent annually (the Federal Reserve Board's target rate).

The 4-percent rule has survived decades of scrutiny, but it does have some caveats. If you retire early, are healthy and your ancestors have lived into their 90s, your retirement may last longer than 30 years. Spending less than 4 percent a year will help preserve your savings. And the 4-percent rule assumes you invest at least half of your portfolio in the stock market, with the remaining money stashed in safer investments such as bonds or CDs. (The process won't work if you invest less than 50 percent in stocks because bond investments will likely earn less.)

To proceed, add up your monthly expenses plus any outlays that hit less often, such as car insurance or property taxes. Use credit card and bank statements to find unusual outlays and estimate which expenses might be higher in retirement, such as travel.

Compare your expected retirement income to your anticipated expenses. If your planned spending would be higher than your income, redo your budget. Can you close the gap by trimming some expenses, such as spacing out longer vacations and filling in with shorter, local trips? Or save a few thousand dollars a year by keeping your car longer?

If possible, delay starting Social Security benefits at least until your full retirement age and, in many cases, until you are 70. As mentioned in chapter 12, delaying until age 70 will boost your monthly benefit 8 percent every year between your full retirement age and 70.

If the gap between income and spending is more like a chasm, think about moving to a cheaper house or even sharing a home with someone, as described in chapter 15. Relocating to a less costly community can ease the stress on your budget. Also consider getting a part-time job to cover a portion of your monthly bills and reduce the amount you draw from savings.

Although these adjustments may be difficult, they are rewarding. You gain peace of mind knowing your spending is in line with your resources and you are unlikely to end up broke.

THE BOND LADDER STRATEGY

What if you stick to your spending plan but your investments are devastated by a stock market crash? During the 2008–2009 financial crisis, the S&P 500 index plunged, losing half its value. Say you had $300,000 in savings. If you had invested half of it in US stocks, your portfolio would have shrunk about $75,000 during those two years.

Such events may tempt you to choose safer but lower returning CDs and bank accounts. But if you skip or sell stocks, you lose out on their higher long-term returns. The key is leaving your stocks untouched during bad times to allow them to rebound.

So how do you keep the cash flowing while you ride out a stock market debacle? It starts with splitting your investments into two parts: equities (stocks or stock mutual funds) and fixed income (bonds, bond mutual funds, CDs, bank accounts). Bert Whitehead, a financial advisor and author, suggests thinking of your equity investments as your crops in the field for future harvests, and your fixed income as the pantry that you tap for your current spending. As long as you keep the crops growing (and don't destroy them in bad times), you will reap ongoing harvests.

Here's how it works. First, "park" about 10 percent of your savings in a money market account for emergencies. Consider using an online bank, such as Ally or Capital One, which may offer a higher interest rate on FDIC-insured savings than your local bank does.

Next, calculate the amount you plan to cash in to cover your spending each year. Say you want to withdraw $12,000 a year. Multiply that number by 10 to figure out how much of your savings to invest in fixed income such as bonds and CDs. Invest the remainder in stocks, preferably in no-load index mutual funds.

So far, this sounds like standard investment advice. But this strategy is not just about diversifying your holdings; it's about safeguarding the money you'll need to tap to pay expenses. A strategy used by Bert Whitehead and members of the organization he founded, the Alliance of Comprehensive Planners, is called a bond ladder. It's a process meant to prevent your savings from running out.

Here's how it works: aim to build a structure (a ladder) comprised of bonds that mature at different times over a 10-year period. Invest enough money in each of these bonds or CDs so that when each one matures, you can use the proceeds to fund your spending. Or you could use those proceeds to reinvest in a bond maturing in 10 years, which would keep the process going.

For example, the first five years of this ladder could contain CDs, each coming due in a subsequent year. Then, to fund the last five years, invest in longer-maturing issues such as Treasury STRIPS— government bonds bought at a discount that reach their full value at maturity. Treasury STRIPS can be purchased in brokerage accounts from companies such as Schwab. You can specify the desired maturity date and the amount you wish to invest.

The beauty of this strategy: as each issue matures, you'll know how much money will become available for spending or reinvesting. And your money is secure. CDs are FDIC-insured up to a total of $250,000 per depositor, per bank, while Treasury STRIPS are widely considered to be the safest investments in the world.

Most years, you'll likely be spending the proceeds of bonds that mature. But if you want to keep the ladder going beyond ten years, you have a couple of options. You can reinvest the proceeds of maturing bonds in new 10-year issues. Or, in years when your stock investments have thrived, you can use profits from the sale of stocks to buy bonds.

To reduce taxes, put your bond ladder in an IRA. In a traditional IRA, earnings won't be taxed until you withdraw the money.

As an alternative to the bond ladder, you could consider a Single Premium Immediate Annuity (SPIA). As described in chapter 9, this product involves paying a lump sum to an insurance company in order to get monthly payments for the rest of your life. For example, according to the calculator at www.immediateannuities.com, if a 65-year-old woman purchased a $150,000 SPIA in 2021, she could expect an immediate payout of about $680 a month for life.

However, the size of your payout depends on when you bought the SPIA. The lower the interest rates at the time of the purchase, the lower your payout will be. And it's locked in. With inflation, the amount you receive now would be worth less in the future.

When you die, the insurance company keeps any money left from your original investment unless you chose an option allowing your beneficiary to receive money after your death. In exchange for providing funds for your beneficiary, you agree to receive a smaller monthly payout.

Generally, the terms of an SPIA cannot be changed once the contract is signed. For some women, the reassurance of the monthly check during their lifetime outweighs the inflexibility of an SPIA. Conversely, a bond ladder strategy can adapt to your situation; you can spend more or less in any given year and still stay on course as long as your average spending is on target.

If you come from a family of long livers and you are concerned your money will run out in your 90s, you might consider purchasing a relatively new type of annuity called a Qualified Longevity Annuity Contract (QLAC). Payouts from this product do not start until you are 85 years old, but you are rewarded for waiting: your monthly check can be as much as six times higher than the payment you would have received at age 65. The extra money could help pay higher health costs or nursing home expenses. Under current rules, you are permitted to invest 25 percent of your retirement nest egg up to $125,000 in a QLAC.

REQUIRED MINIMUM DISTRIBUTIONS

The money you contributed to your retirement accounts cannot stay there indefinitely. No later than December 31 of the year you turn 72 (under current rules) and each year thereafter, you must withdraw a portion of your traditional IRAs and other retirement plans except Roth IRAs and Roth 401(k)s. The amount you must withdraw is called a Required Minimum Distribution (RMD).

Companies holding your IRA calculate the amount of your annual RMD. But to compute it on your own: divide the balance in the account on December 31 of the previous year by your age factor (listed in the Uniform Lifetime Table found on the IRS website [www.irs. gov]). As an example, if you are 72 in 2021, and your IRA was worth $100,000 on December 31, 2020, your RMD for 2021 totals $3,906.50 ($100,000 divided by your 25.6 age factor). If you want help, use calculators on www.dinkytown.net to compute your RMD. *Note:* The RMD is the smallest amount you must take out of your retirement plans; of course, you can withdraw a larger sum in any given year.

You'll be taxed at your regular income tax rate on your withdrawal. But if you fail to take out the required amount, the IRS can charge you a penalty of 50 percent of the missed withdrawal.

EARLY RETIREMENT

Retiring in your 50s or early 60s requires extra planning. Unless you're receiving disability benefits, Medicare isn't available until age 65 even if you started drawing Social Security retirement benefits earlier. If you retire before age 65, you may be able to stay on your employer's health insurance plan for 18 months postretirement via a provision called COBRA. To qualify, you must have worked for state or local government or a private employer that has at least 20 employees and have been enrolled in your employer's plan before you retired. Generally, you pay the full health insurance premium plus a small administrative fee. Since many employers subsidize your health insurance while you work, your premium is likely to jump once you're on COBRA.

As an alternative to COBRA, shop for your own policy on the Health Insurance Marketplace (HIM) (www.healthcare.gov). HIM plans cover preexisting conditions, and you cannot be denied coverage. If your income is lower than $51,040 (for a single person in 2021), you qualify for a tax credit that effectively lowers your monthly premium. For example, due to her modest income, a retired 60-year-old female with a $31,000 income qualifies for a $608 per month tax credit in 2021. Thus, her tax credit reduces her monthly premium by $608, and her HIM plan may also entitle her to lower copays and deductibles than she would pay with a non-HIM plan.

You can buy health insurance through a broker. But, to capture a tax credit and other HIM benefits, be sure to sign up for coverage at www.healthcare.gov or on the website of your state's insurance marketplace. If you opt to continue coverage under COBRA, you can shop for an individual policy 18 months later, when your COBRA eligibility ends.

Three months before you turn 65, apply for Medicare either online at www.ssa.gov or in person at a Social Security office. If you wait longer than three months after age 65 to sign up, you will pay a late enrollment penalty every month.

As described in chapter 12, the higher your income, the more you will pay for Medicare Parts B and D. If you have been paying higher premiums for Medicare and your income drops when you retire, Medicare will adjust your premium about two years later. To speed up the process, you can apply for an immediate reduction by filing form SSA-44 (available at www.ssa.gov).

An additional dilemma facing early retirees: if you are younger than 59½, how can you avoid paying the 10 percent penalty—on top of regular income tax—on money you withdraw from IRAs or retirement plans? You have a few options: you don't pay a penalty if you are disabled or you use the money to pay education costs or medical bills that total more than 7½ percent of your income. Money withdrawn from an Inherited IRA is also penalty-free—at any age. If you retired at age 55 or later, you may be able to tap your 401(k) plan penalty-free.

Roth IRAs are more flexible: you can withdraw an amount equal to the money you contributed any time, penalty- and tax-free. You can withdraw any amount penalty- and tax-free when you are 59½ or older if your first Roth IRA contribution occurred at least five years ago.

You can also escape the 10 percent penalty if you set up regular withdrawals from your IRA—called "substantially equal periodic payments." The rules are tricky, so it's best to consult a financial planner or tax advisor for help with this strategy.

ROTH IRA CONVERSIONS

When your paychecks stop, you can no longer contribute to a Roth or a traditional IRA. But you can transfer funds any time from a traditional IRA to a Roth IRA. Five years after you moved this money—or any time, if you are 59 ½ or older—you can withdraw the transferred funds tax- and penalty-free from your Roth IRA. Of course, you'll pay taxes on any money you transfer to a Roth from a traditional IRA.

So why go this route? It could provide tax advantages if you're in a lower tax bracket now than you expect to be later. Right now, you'll pay taxes on the transferred amount at your current tax rate. But later, when your tax rate is higher, you'll be able to withdraw the money tax-free. A good strategy to consider: transfer money to a Roth IRA early in retirement, before you have to take RMD withdrawals from your retirement plans (at age 72). But, before transferring money, determine how much extra in taxes a transfer will cost. To do so, ask your tax preparer or use a calculator on a site such as www.dinkytown.net.

MANAGING YOUR RETIREMENT ACCOUNTS

What will you do with money in your 401(k) plan when you retire? You can leave it in the plan if your account is worth at least $5,000. Or you can roll the money into your IRA. There are advantages to the latter:

- In an IRA, your investment choices are not restricted to the list offered by the 401(k) provider. You can search for low-cost investments such as index funds or ETFs or expand your horizons and invest in socially responsible (ESG) funds.

- You can convert all or part of your IRA into a Roth IRA.
- After age 70½, you can contribute to charities with tax-free withdrawals from your IRA via a Qualified Charitable Distribution (QCD).
- If you have money in more than one employer's retirement plan, you can streamline your investments by rolling all your retirement accounts into a single IRA.
- If your money is in an IRA, and you want some of it annuitized—converted to monthly payments—you can purchase an annuity from any insurance company you choose.

To avoid paying taxes on the money you roll into your IRA, make sure the plan transfers the money directly to your IRA and not to you personally. If the money is mistakenly sent to you, it will be taxed unless you transfer it to your IRA within 60 calendar days.

If you enlist the help of an advisor to roll over your retirement plans, choose a fiduciary—a professional who is required to act in your best interest. Many financial advisors who are fiduciaries charge a flat fee or hourly rate. Nonfiduciary brokers or salespersons can charge commissions as high as 9 percent on money you roll over from a retirement plan.

14

ESTATE AND ELDER PLANNING

You may think it's too soon. The last thing you want to deal with if you're say, younger than 60, is planning for old age or death. But this process, called estate planning, is a necessity. And it must be done immediately if you have children, since you never know when something could happen to you.

Essentially, estate planning, and its cousin, elder planning, map what will happen if you become incapacitated or die. They also entail preparing for events that could have devastating consequences, especially if you're living alone. For instance: Who will care for you if you become ill? Who can you trust to handle your finances if you are incapacitated? And the thorniest of the existential questions: Who would make end-of-life decisions if you are unable to do so?

These are just some of the crucial issues involved with estate planning. Solo life can be liberating—you make your own choices—but without planning ahead, you can't be sure who would help you in an emergency—who could rush to your side if you suddenly were injured or fell sick.

As the population ages, such issues will become ever more prevalent. But they may be impacting many people already. Indeed, in 2018, almost a third of women ages 65 through 74 lived by themselves, according to *Older Americans 2020*, a chart book published by the Federal Interagency Forum on Aging Related Statistics. That same year, more than 44 percent of women 85 and older lived alone—almost twice the percentage of men.[1]

But single women don't need to fear the future. By making longer-term choices now—or at least by the time you're in your 60s—you can arrange for a more comfortable life ahead while gaining peace of mind in the present. And you should feel gratified: by taking such steps as creating a will and designating beneficiaries, you will help support the people, and perhaps organizations, who mean the most to you.

How to move forward? Although the steps aren't necessarily complicated, they involve some soul-searching. Timewise, you should prioritize your estate planning and then pursue elder planning—researching where you could live and what services you could access.

ESTATE PLANNING ESSENTIALS

According to Matt Gibson, an attorney in Columbus, Ohio, all single women need, at minimum, a will, a durable power of attorney (for financial matters) and a durable health care power of attorney. Other documents, such as a living will or trust, may also be appropriate.

In fact, single women need to take extra care with their estate plan, the attorney says. That's because your wishes may not be known or honored unless spelled out in signed legal documents. In contrast, if you're married, a physician will likely allow your spouse to make decisions about your health care if you are unable to do so.

The people you name in your estate documents will be those you most cherish and trust. Before choosing them, discuss their role in your estate plan and obtain their approval.

Your Will

Your last will and testament is a legal document that names your heirs, the guardians for any children who are minors and the executor who carries out the terms of your will. Your executor makes sure any taxes and final expenses are paid and your assets are divided according to your wishes, as you state them in your will.

Although you identify heirs to your estate in your will, beneficiaries named to specific accounts, such as an IRA, take precedence: your beneficiary inherits the account no matter what your will states. As an example, if you named your friend Sherry the beneficiary of your IRA, but your will specifies that your entire estate goes to your niece Olivia, Sherry will inherit your IRA.

When creating a will, remember to sign it in front of two witnesses; they will also sign the document. Also explore whether, in your state, you should create a notarized self-proving affidavit, which attests to the validity of the will and can streamline the probate process.

Power of Attorney

Naming a person—or persons—to make decisions about your finances and property on your behalf is a critical piece of your estate plan. You do this with a power-of-attorney document. Unless you specifically limit this power of attorney, it typically grants broad powers to the person you designate. These include the ability to pay bills, manage financial accounts, gift money and change account beneficiaries on your behalf. A "durable" power of attorney can give the designee these rights immediately, and they remain in effect if you become incapacitated. Be sure to name someone you trust, given the importance of this role. In contrast, a "springing" power of attorney does not take effect until a specific event occurs, such as a determination by one or more doctors that you are incapacitated. You may need witnesses or a notarized signature on your power-of-attorney document, depending on your state's laws.

Medical Power of Attorney and Living Will

The medical power of attorney appoints someone you choose to make decisions about your health care if you cannot make or communicate them. Some decisions may include whether to perform surgery if you are unconscious, say, due to a severe accident, or to continue life support if your condition is judged to be terminal.

A living will, sometimes called an advance or medical directive, specifies your choices for end-of-life care. Typically, it states whether you wish to receive life-sustaining treatment if you are terminally ill or in a permanently unconscious state. When executing a living will, make sure the document conforms to the rules of your state, including whether your signature needs to be notarized and/or witnessed.

Trust

The addition of a trust may provide additional protection and flexibility to your estate plan. A trust is simply a legal entity that holds assets you put into it. It is managed by a trustee—an individual or institution—on behalf of the trust's beneficiaries. During your lifetime, the arrangement is called a "living" or "revocable" trust, which allows you to change, or even cancel, the trust. Many individuals serve as their own trustees during their lifetime and name one or more successor trustees to take over if they become incapacitated or at their death. Your trust becomes "irrevocable" when you die, and it cannot be changed. Some complex estate plans involve the use of an irrevocable trust during your lifetime.

Whether a trust is appropriate for you depends on your situation. Some reasons to consider drafting a trust include:

- You wish to expedite the process of turning over management of your affairs if you should become incapacitated. The successor trustee can step in for you and handle any accounts or property in the trust.
- You want to avoid probate, a legal process that can be both lengthy and expensive. Assets in a trust will be distributed directly to your beneficiaries without going through probate. *Note:* Naming beneficiaries to your accounts, such as your IRA and bank account, also avoids probate. Some states also allow you to avoid probate by adding a beneficiary to the title of your home.
- You wish to be able to provide detailed instructions about who gets what in your estate. As an example, you may wish to create an education fund for family members, with instructions for how much will be earmarked for college. Or, after designating spe-

cific bequests to individuals, you may stipulate that any remaining funds go to charity.

- You wish to provide funds for a disabled individual without jeopardizing any government benefits the individual is receiving. These special-purpose instructions, often called "special needs trusts," should be prepared by an attorney knowledgeable on the subject.

Given the importance of your estate plan, you should carefully select the people involved—the executor of your will, your power-of-attorney designees, and trustees and guardian, if applicable. Ideally, they should live nearby, be younger than you, and, in the case of the power-of-attorney designee, have some grasp of finances. For your health care or medical power of attorney, choose a caring relative or friend who understands your wishes for end-of-life care and, preferably, has worked in health care.

You can also name your lawyer to be your power of attorney, executor or trustee, or you may ask a bank to serve as your trustee. You or your estate will pay fees for this service.

PREPARING YOUR DOCUMENTS

Who should draft your estate-planning documents? Working with an attorney is advisable if your finances or family situation are complicated. And you may decide to hire an attorney to draft your plan to ensure your wishes are properly reflected in your documents and you have not made an error that could cause hardship for your heirs. Ask two or three local estate-planning attorneys to quote you a fee for a will and power of attorney. You can save money by downloading templates for a health care power of attorney and living will from a local hospital's website or by contacting your state's chapter of the American Bar Association.

Alternatively, you can purchase software that will guide you through the process of drafting your documents. On the internet, you can find an array of will-making services whose costs range from nothing to $100 or more. These tools can be handy and quick if the terms of your will are simple.

However you get your documents written and signed, do it soon: you never know when you'll need them.

HOUSING AND SERVICES IN OLDER AGE

Where do you think you'll want to live in old age? And how will you make that happen, especially when you're less agile than you are today? These are tough decisions and should involve family members, friends and professionals, such as an attorney or financial advisor.

Most seniors over 50 years of age—76 percent, according to research by AARP[2]—want to stay in their current home. To ensure that happens, you need to explore options, ideally before retirement. Services you'll likely need may range from meal delivery to transportation to health care. Investigate how you would obtain such services when the need arises. Check what's available in your area. For help, contact your local elected officials or community organizations, or visit the US Administration on Aging's "Eldercare Locator," at https:// eldercare.acl.gov.

Home Health Care

This option is often desirable but pricey. According to Genworth Financial, a long-term care insurance provider, in 2020 the cost of a home health aide working about six hours a day totaled more than $4,600 a month in Columbus, Ohio.[3] (And this figure doesn't include your standard living expenses, such as rent or mortgage, groceries and utilities.) If you live in a more expensive city, such as San Francisco, the monthly home-care bill for the same six hours a day can top $6,200. And the bill will be at least double for around-the-clock care.

You can also get help at home from a retirement community. Many of these businesses now offer a "hybrid" option: for an up-front charge of around $50,000 and then a monthly fee of several hundred dollars, you get help at home when you need it. But plan ahead on two counts: (1) at the time you apply for this option, you must be able to live on your own with little or no assistance; and (2) you must have enough income and savings to cover the monthly fee, sometimes for years before you need the services.

Retirement Communities

Consider this setting if you think you'll worry about living at home alone in old age and you enjoy being around other people and participating in planned activities. One option to consider is a continuing care retirement community, or CCRC. As the name implies, this type of facility offers a range of care, from independent living to assisted living to skilled nursing and, in many cases, specialized memory care. To be approved to live at a CCRC, you must pass three hurdles: (1) be at least 62 years old, (2) be healthy enough to live on your own (independently) and (3) have sufficient investments, savings and income. The financial requirements vary by community. In some facilities, for instance, a female between the ages of 75 and 79 must have savings and investments, plus 12.44 years of Social Security and/ or pension benefits, totaling at least $900,000. In this hypothetical example, if you are 76 years old and receive $30,000 a year from Social Security and a pension, you would need $526,800 in savings to qualify. One way to cover that cost would be to sell your home.

If you choose a CCRC, your charges will likely include: an entrance fee between $100,000 and $1 million, and monthly fees of between $2,000 and $8,000, depending on the community's location and its services. If you move out or die, a portion of your entrance fee may be refundable to you or your heirs.

Although expensive, CCRCs cover many day-to-day living needs and costs. Typically, they offer at least one meal a day along with access to such activities as guest lectures, classes and trips to local cultural events. Another draw: if you can afford the costliest CCRC option—the life-care model—you'll be able to stay in the community even if you deplete your assets.

Alternatively, if you can't afford CCRCs' substantial entry fee, you could consider their rental option. Although the monthly fee is higher than the cost of a life-care CCRC facility, there's no up-front cost. You will pay as you go for any extra help, such as for a caregiver who assists with activities such as bathing or dressing.

Before choosing a retirement community, visit it. Tour the facilities, including the assisted living and skilled nursing units, talk to residents and participate in an activity. Ask the director about fee increases in recent years and staff turnover. But don't race to sign up. Check to see if the retirement community has been accredited by CARF, a nonprofit accreditor of health and human services. CARF also publishes a useful guide on its website (www.carf.org) containing a list of questions to ask when evaluating a community.[4] And before signing any contracts, discuss the facility and its cost with your attorney or financial planner.

Community-Based Group Homes and Co-Housing

Community-based group homes have been increasingly popular with seniors. Residents in these smaller arrangements enjoy a homey ambiance and lower monthly fees compared to a full-service retirement community. And they are widespread. As of the fall of 2020, one such provider, the nonprofit Greenhouse Project (www.thegreen houseproject.org), had over 300 such homes in 32 states.

If you wish to share housing costs with other single women—even well before older age—consider co-housing. Groups such as the nonprofit Co-Housing Association of the United States (www.cohousing .org) provide information on creating and maintaining co-housing arrangements. Another resource, Women for Living in Community (www.womenlivingincommunity.com), guides you on how to locate shared housing and other alternatives to retirement communities.

Perhaps you have decided where you would eventually like to live. Now the key question is, Will you be able to afford it? Some options, along with your savings and Social Security income, include:

- Medicare: Although not a long-term solution, Medicare provides some coverage for care. Generally, Medicare Part A will pay for up to 20 days of skilled nursing services in a certified facility after a hospital stay lasting at least 3 days. For days 21 through 100, you're charged $185.50 a day (in 2021), and Medicare pays the rest. However, if you have supplemental insurance (sometimes called "Medigap" coverage), your policy will cover the daily $185.50 fee. And many policies pay 80 percent of an additional 80 days in a nursing facility.

- Veteran's benefits: If you are a veteran or the surviving spouse of a veteran, you may receive a monthly benefit to pay for your care through the Veterans Administration's Aid and Assistance or Homebound programs. To qualify, you must be 65 or older, you or your spouse must have served in the military and your assets—minus any outstanding loans—must total less than $130,773 (as of December 2020). Apply on the US Department of Veterans Affairs' website (www.va.gov) or seek help from an attorney or advisor who specializes in veterans' benefits.

- Medicaid. If you have depleted your funds, Medicaid may cover all or part of your costs in a skilled nursing facility. But relying on it may limit your choices, since many nursing homes ration the spaces, or "beds," available to Medicaid recipients. Because Medicaid is state administered, where you live determines both your eligibility and your application process. Some states also allow Medicaid to fund in-home services or assisted-living care in retirement communities. You can check for these Medicaid waiver programs at www.medicaid.gov.

- Long-term care (LTC) insurance. This may be an option if you can afford the hefty premiums—and if you are healthy enough to qualify. To help gauge the cost, use an online cost-of-care calculator such as the one provided by Genworth, an insurance provider (www.genworth.com). Consider this example: in 2021 a 65-year-old woman would spend more than $2,400 a year for a policy that will pay $125 a day (about half the daily cost of a nursing home) for three years, after a 90-day waiting period.[5] Adding an inflation rider will increase the premium. But bear in mind: you may be denied coverage if you have preexisting health conditions. If you are considering purchasing LTC coverage, shop around for quotes. A rule of thumb: don't allocate more than 5 percent of your budget on these premiums. Since you may never need this coverage, spending more than 5 percent on it could limit your funds for other purposes. The premium you pay for LTC coverage is not locked in; on occasion, some insurance companies have levied double-digit increases. If you are faced with a big jump in your premium, consider reducing your coverage: pare the daily benefit or number of years of coverage or cancel the annual inflation adjustment.

Relying on Family

To be sure, you may be hoping to avoid wading through all these choices and costs. In the back of your mind, you may expect relatives to assist you in later life. And you wouldn't be alone. According to a study published by the AARP Public Policy Institute, 68 percent of Americans believe they will be able to rely on family members as they age.[6] But you'd be unwise to count on that, since relatives may not be willing or available to help when the time comes. The same AARP study states the ratio of potential family caregivers to those needing care is expected to slide from seven caregivers for each 80-plus senior in 2010 to four caregivers in 2030, when baby boomers hit their 80s. Hence this advice: Sure, seek help. But also do your own planning.

15

HELP IN HARD TIMES

Several years ago, financial planner Charles Failla was dining in New York City with a client and two of his friends when the conversation took a grim turn. The topic was suicide in the military. According to an article one diner had read, some destitute soldiers had taken their lives so their families could apply for a death benefit.

That disclosure hit hard. "It brought tears to my eyes," since these people had been serving their country, recalled Charles Failla, founder and principal of Sovereign Financial Group.

He resolved to help. About a year and a half later, at his request, he became a director of a Connecticut chapter of the Financial Planning Association (FPA), with the intention of restarting the group's pro bono financial advisory service. The free offering would be targeted to people of lower to moderate income who typically can't afford a financial advisor.

The revived Connecticut offering—today one of the many FPA pro bono programs nationwide—began in 2018 with in-person presentations on personal finance and went virtual in 2020. The way it works: volunteer financial planners from around the state provide the instruction, and typically local community groups refer people to the program. They have a pressing need for such guidance. "Many people find it difficult to make ends meet since their income barely covers their basic needs," observes Charles Failla, who heads the Pro Bono/ Public Outreach Committee of what is now the Connecticut FPA chapter.

And these folks seeking help are hardly alone. In a United States where millions of people are either poor, unemployed, coping with a disaster or living one lost paycheck away from destitution, services such as the FPA's can be a lifeline.

Many other public and private organizations are similarly lending a hand.

In this chapter, you'll find listings of programs that provide help in a range of areas. Categories include housing, food, eldercare and childcare, education and job search, legal, health and general needs. Sources range from government entities to nonprofit organizations to businesses. Although this section doesn't cover the landscape of offerings, it highlights an array of valuable programs that are free or affordable.

GENERAL HELP

2-1-1 Helpline. If you're unsure where to seek local help with an issue or problem, dial 2-1-1. That free, 24-hour helpline connects you to a trained specialist who can refer you to a local organization or service that can address your concern. Issues can include housing, food, health care, insurance assistance, utilities payments, employment services, veterans' and family services, suicide prevention and more, according to the website of United Way (www.unitedway.org), which supports 2-1-1. You can dial the number from a landline or mobile phone, or visit www.211.org for additional contact options. The line is open to anyone and can be used as often as needed.

FINANCIAL ADVICE

The **Financial Planning Association** (**FPA**) engages in three separate, pro bono financial advisory programs on an ongoing basis. These include the 86 local chapters and two state councils that provide free financial advice to lower-income individuals and groups in their area; financial advice to cancer patients; and financial guidance to participants in the Homes for Our Troops program:

- Pro bono financial advisory program. In this program, local FPA chapters across the country—such as the FPA of Connecticut—create their own content and scheduling. Volunteer financial planners conduct the programs. While specific offerings can vary, the overall aim is to provide financial guidance to help those in need "build assets and improve their lives," says Kurt Kaczor, FPA director of pro bono. To find an FPA chapter offering pro bono financial advice, visit www.financialplanningassociation. org, click "Lead" and then click "Pro Bono."
- Financial planning for cancer patients and their families. The FPA provides this service in partnership with the organizations Family Reach and the Foundation for Financial Planning. Advice from FPA volunteers focuses on financially managing cancer treatments and other costs. For information on obtaining this service, visit www.familyreach.org.
- Homes for Our Troops. This program provides specially adapted custom homes for severely wounded post-9/11 veterans. FPA volunteers work with recipients to ensure they can meet the financial requirements of home ownership. For information on Homes for Our Troops, go to www.hfotusa.org.

Savvy Ladies (www.savvyladies.org) offers a wealth of financial resources for women. Among the nonprofit's free offerings are its webinars, Helpline, online budgeting tools, online debt course and articles.

Through its Helpline, women can have a one-time free phone consultation with a volunteer financial expert. Although topics can cover any financial issue, common questions and concerns center on debt, savings and divorce-related issues, says Lisa Ernst, former executive director of SavvyLadies.

Webinars cover a broad swath of topics, ranging from student loans to family finances, kids and divorce and more. There's also an online, six-week Dominate Your Debt course and a calculator that computes your finance charges on unpaid credit card balances.

Need help creating a budget? Try SavvyLadies' free worksheets to help you tally and compare your income against expenses on a 1-month or 12-month basis.

Other Helpful Sites for Women

Among other informative internet sites targeted to women are the **Women's Institute for a Secure Retirement** (www.wiserwomen .org), the **Women's Institute for Financial Education** (www .WIFE.org), the **Institute for Women's Policy Research** (www .iwpr.org), the **National Women's Law Center** (www.nwlcorg), the National Partnership for Women and Families (www.nationalpartner ship.org), the **American Association of University Women** (www .aauw.org) and **Moms Rising** (www.momsrising.org).

If You Need Funds . . .

The nonprofit **Modest Needs** (www.modestneeds.org) provides grants to working people in the United States and Canada who have a sudden need for money to pay bills they can't afford. Needs typically include an unexpected emergency or a monthly bill that becomes un-affordable due to unforeseen circumstances, such as a mother taking unpaid leave from work to care for a sick child.

As its target audience, Modest Needs helps people with incomes slightly above the federal poverty line (an annual income of $12,760 for one individual in 2020), since they may not qualify for certain antipoverty programs, explains Keith Taylor, CEO at Modest Needs Foundation.

To seek a grant, file an online, no-cost application on www.modest needs.org; approved requests will then be posted on that website to attract donors through the crowdfunding process. Grants are made directly to vendors, not to applicants, and cannot be paid using cash or gift certificates. Each grant averages between $750 and $1,250 and doesn't need to be repaid. For additional information, visit www .modestneeds.org.

Temporary Assistance to Needy Families (TANF). The TANF program provides eligible needy families with cash for a limited time and may offer noncash benefits, such as job training. To qualify, you must be pregnant or responsible for a child younger than 19, have a low or very low income and be underemployed, unemployed or about to become unemployed, according to Benefits.gov. Funding goes from federal grants to state and territories, which, in turn, set eligibility requirements and benefits. To find where to apply in your state, territory or tribe, visit www.acf.hhs.gov/programs/ofa/help.

Supplemental Security Income (SSI). SSI is a federal income-supplement program financed by general tax revenues, with payments administered by the Social Security Administration (SSA). According to the SSA, the program helps disabled adults and children who have limited income and resources. It also can serve non-disabled people ages 65 and older if they meet the financial limits. The program, which has strict income limits, provides cash to pay basic needs, including food, clothing and shelter. For help determining whether you qualify, check the Benefit Eligibility Screening Tool at www.ssabest .benefits.gov. For more information on SSI, visit www.ssa.gov and search for Supplemental Security Income.

Unemployment Insurance. If you lose your job through no fault of your own, you'll want to apply for unemployment benefits as soon as possible. According to the US Department of Labor, unemployment insurance, a joint federal-state program, provides cash benefits to eligible workers. Each state sets its own rules for qualifications, including time worked and salary earned. For information on filing for unemployment benefits in your state, go online to www.careerone stop.org.

Tax Preparation

The IRS provides free help with tax preparation for those who qualify through its **Volunteer Income Tax Assistance** (VITA) and **Tax Counseling for the Elderly** (TCE) programs.

You may be eligible for the VITA program if you earn about $56,000 a year or less, have a disability, are elderly or speak limited English. The TCE program, which is mainly targeted to those ages 60 and older, "specializes in questions about pensions and retirement-related issues." The IRS-certified volunteers who provide tax counseling are often retired individuals associated with nonprofit organizations. For more information, visit www.irs.gov and search for Free Tax Preparation Near You.

HOUSING ASSISTANCE

If you can't pay your rent or mortgage, inquire about some payment relief, however temporary, from your landlord or mortgage lender. Or you could also ask family or friends for a loan. Longer-term solutions (that don't involve government assistance) could include downsizing to smaller, cheaper quarters or taking in a housemate.

The latter, called shared housing, includes renting space in your home or becoming a renter in someone else's home. And the benefits of it aren't just financial, suggests Annamarie Pluhar, founder and president of the nonprofit **Sharing Housing Inc.**, which provides education and advocacy for shared housing. "A key component of shared housing is the companionship it provides," says Annamarie, who is also author of the book *Sharing Housing: A Guidebook for Finding and Keeping Good Housemates*. Sharing Housing (https://sharinghousing.com) provides online courses on shared housing; its informational blog and worksheets are free.

Consumers wishing to share a home can find matching services that are both for-profit and not-for-profit. A directory of such not-for-profit services can be found at www.nationalsharedhousing.org, the website of the National Shared Housing Resources Center.

Housing Help from the Government

The federal **Department of Housing and Urban Development** (HUD) addresses housing needs of Americans in a range of programs, from mortgage and loan assistance to community development to rental assistance, homeless assistance and more. For low-income people, the three major rental assistance programs provided by HUD programs are (1) subsidized housing in privately owned buildings, (2) public housing and (3) the Housing Choice Voucher Program. As briefly explained by HUD:

- Subsidized housing in privately owned buildings involves the government paying landlords to offer reduced rents to low-income tenants. To participate, you would search for an apartment (you can use the online HUD Resource Locator at resources.hud.gov) and apply directly at the building's management office.
- Public housing consists of affordable apartments or rental houses for low-income families, the elderly and persons with disabilities. To apply, contact your local housing authority or agency. To find it online, visit www.hud.gov and search for PHA contact information, or use the HUD Resource Locator.
- The Housing Choice Voucher Program enables you to find a rental property and use the voucher to pay for all or part of the rent. Apply for the voucher program through your local housing authority.

To find possible housing assistance from your state and local governments or other organizations, visit www.hud.gov and search for the HUD Resource Locator. For information on local homeless shelters, visit the same website and click the "Find Shelter" tool.

For rural Americans, the **US Department of Agriculture** (USDA) provides homeownership opportunities and home renovation and repair programs, according to USDA.gov. That department also provides financing to disabled, elderly or low-income rural residents in multiunit housing complexes to ensure that they can pay their rent. For information, visit www.usda.gov and search for "housing assistance."

If your income is low and you need help with energy bills, consider the **Low-Income Home Energy Assistance Program** (LIHEAP). This federally funded program can help eligible households with the cost of heating and cooling, weatherization and energy-related home repairs. For more information, visit www.acf.hhs.gov/ocs/programs /liheap.

FOOD ASSISTANCE

Among the main governmental sources of food assistance:

The federal **Supplemental Nutrition Assistance Program** (SNAP), formerly known as food stamps, is the nation's largest provider of food assistance targeted to low-income people. The majority of recipients are children, seniors or disabled people. SNAP recipients pay for food on a debit-like card that is automatically filled monthly. To apply for benefits, contact your local SNAP office. You can find the SNAP Directory of Resources at www.fns.usda.gov. Bear in mind that the SNAP program entails work requirements (which have been temporarily suspended during the coronavirus pandemic). For details on these requirements, visit www.fns.usda.gov/SNAP /work-requirements.

The **Special Supplemental Nutrition Programs for Women, Infants and Children** (WIC) provides nutritious foods to supplement diets as well as nutrition education and referrals to other health and social services, according to the USDA. This short-term food/ nutrition program serves low-income women who are pregnant, postpartum, or breastfeeding and infants and children up to age five who are nutritionally at risk. To learn more, visit www.fns.usda.gov/wic.

The federally assisted **National School Lunch Program** provides free or reduced-cost lunches to children who qualify. Lunches are free for children from families with incomes at 130 percent of the federal poverty line or lower. Children in households with incomes between 130 percent and 185 percent of poverty can receive reduced-price lunches. How to apply? According to the USDA, schools send home applications for school meals at the beginning of the school year. But parents may apply during the year for their children by requesting and submitting an application to the children's school or district.

Beyond government programs, nonprofit organizations, community groups and food pantries can provide help. For instance, the nonprofit **Feeding America** supports 200 food banks, 60,000 food pantries and meal programs. It serves one in seven Americans who need food. Generally, showing up at a food distribution site or requesting help is proof enough of need, according to officials of Feeding America. To find a local food bank, visit www.feedingamerica.org/find-your-local -foodbank. Feeding America's food banks can help you find a feeding program in your community.

Additionally, you can search online for local food pantries at www .foodpantries.org. Or call 2-1-1 to find local organizations providing food to those in need.

LEGAL HELP

If your income is low and you need legal help with a civil matter, consider seeking assistance from a legal aid organization. The feder-ally financed **Legal Services Corporation** (LSC) provides funding for 132 legal aid organizations with more than 800 offices nation-wide. Legal aid offices typically handle concerns involving housing, consumer issues, public benefits and family law issues such as child support and custody and domestic violence. Fully 70 percent of legal aid clients are women. Applicants should have annual household in-comes at or below 125 percent of the federal poverty line. However, middle-income people who lose their job may be able to qualify for LSC-funded help. If your civil case is accepted, your legal services will be free. But be aware that most legal aid offices get more requests for help than they can handle, says an LSC spokesperson.

To find a local LSC-funded program online, visit www.LSC.gov and search on the "Find Legal Aid" page. The affiliated website www. LawHelp.org provides an array of legal information and forms you can download for free.

The **American Bar Association** (ABA) offers www.findlegalhelp .org, which provides a variety of resources if you cannot afford a law-yer, including links to legal aid and pro bono organization directories. The ABA also offers ABA Free Legal Answers for those unable to af-ford a lawyer who need answers to their legal questions. To access this virtual legal clinic, visit www.abafreelegalanswers.org. After locating your home state from the dropdown menu, fill out a form and then post a civil legal question for a volunteer lawyer. All correspondence takes place on the Free Legal Answers site; you receive an email when your legal question has been answered.

Are you facing sex discrimination or sexual harassment at work, in school or as a patient obtaining health care? The **National Women's Law Center** (NWLC) may be able to help. Its Legal Network for Gender Equity program can provide contact information for three attorneys in your area who can handle such cases. Attorneys in the network offer a free initial consultation. To access this service, visit www.nwlc.org/legalhelp.

If your case involves sexual harassment at work, and you can't afford legal counsel, your attorney can apply to the NWLC TIME'S UP Legal Defense Fund for financial help with your legal costs. The fund supports selected cases of workplace sexual harassment, reports Sharyn Tejani, director of the TIME'S UP Legal Defense Fund and the Legal Network for Gender Equity. Attorneys can apply for funding at www.nwlc.org/timesupfundingapp.

ELDERCARE AND CHILDCARE

The **Eldercare Locator** (https://eldercare.acl.gov), a public service of the US Administration on Aging, offers a wealth of resources and contacts relating to the care of seniors. Its online search tool links to local organizations providing assistance to older adults. The Eldercare Locator also can be reached by phone at 800-677-1116.

Among its other features, the Eldercare Locator provides separate pages of information and resources for seniors on support services, housing, elder rights, insurance and benefits, health and transportation. Its "Caregiver Corner" features information and resources for caregivers, while its "Helpful Links" section identifies (with website links) federal and nongovernmental organizations that address aging issues, health and disease-specific resources and end-of-life resources.

When seeking childcare services, you'll find no shortage of internet sites offering information. One good place to start would be **Child Care.gov**. This site, operated by the US Department of Health and Human Services, Administration for Children and Families, Office of Child Care, provides a search tool with links to childcare services in your state. In addition, its pages of information cover an array of topics, among them, care options, ways to ensure safe and healthy childcare, choosing quality care and paying for care.

EDUCATION AND JOB SEARCH

If you scrape by on low wages or are unemployed or saddled with a miserable work situation, you likely want new or better employment. Or perhaps a whole new career. But how to make that happen?

Luckily, groups from charities to big corporations to labor unions have been stepping up, offerings services from recruitment programs and apprenticeships to job boards, mentoring and networking for women.

The **CareerOneStop** website (www.careeronestop.org), sponsored by the US Labor Department, has a plethora of materials to help job seekers. Its free resources cover such topics as job search information, job training, details on careers and workforce resources in your area.

Features include tutorials on writing resumes and preparing for job interviews. Also available are tools to help compare salaries across industries and locations, listings of job banks and free classes for basic academic and computer skills. The site also delves into specific topics, such as returning to work; changing careers; self-employment; resources for transitioning service members, workers with disabilities, older and younger workers; and more.

Among the programs of the **American Association of University Women** (AAUW) are its Career Development Grants and its American Fellowships programs:

- Career Development Grants help women pursuing a certificate or degree advance their careers, change careers or reenter the workforce in the fields of health care, education, medical science or social science. Grants currently range from $2,000 to $12,000 and can cover tuition, books, transportation and dependent care.

• AAUW's American Fellowships help women pursuing full-time study to complete a dissertation, conduct postdoctoral research or prepare research for publication for eight consecutive weeks. Candidates must be US citizens or permanent residents. Funds range from $6,000 to $30,000. For information on the AAUW programs, visit www.aauw.org.

The Live Your Dream: Education and Training Awards for Women is a program of **Soroptimist**, an organization whose volunteers provide women and girls with access to education and training. The Live Your Dream Awards total more than $2.8 million annually and are for women who have faced domestic violence, the death of a spouse, substance abuse or other problems. The awards cover any costs of higher education, such as books, childcare, tuition and transportation, and start at approximately $1,000 (award amounts vary locally) up to $16,000 total. To be eligible, you need to be the primary financial support of your household and in financial need, and to have applied to or been accepted at a vocational or undergraduate program. To apply, visit www.soroptimist.org; applications are accepted between August 1 and November 15 each year.

If you're seeking a career in the trades, check the website of **Nontraditional Employment for Women** (www.new-nyc.org). The New York nonprofit trains and places women in "non-traditional careers in the building and construction trades, public utilities, transportation, green jobs and building maintenance and operation—jobs that provide structured career pathways to the middle class and economic independence," its website states. NEW has core training programs that are offered during the day and evening. You can enroll online.

Other major cities around the country have similar organizations, such as the Chicago Women in Trades and California's Tradeswomen, Inc.

The **US Small Business Administration's (SBA) Office of Women's Business Ownership** runs programs at its district offices around the country to offer business training and counseling, access to credit and capital and marketing opportunities, including federal contracts. It helps women entrepreneurs, especially those who historically have been underserved or excluded, per the SBA website. Among the SBA's programs are its Women's Business Centers, which help women-owned businesses line up funds and compete for federal contracts that are set aside for minority- and women-owned businesses. For more information, visit www.sba.gov/women.

For entrepreneurs, the financial firm **Goldman Sachs** offers programs titled 10,000 Women and 10,000 Small Businesses.

- 10,000 Women provides female entrepreneurs with business education, mentoring and networking opportunities and access to capital. Its free online course is available to any female entrepreneur around the world. The program consists of 10 courses covering such business topics as marketing, finance and operations. You can take any course or a combination of them. To enroll, visit www.coursera.org/launch/10000women.

- 10,000 Small Businesses provides business education, support services and access to capital for growth-oriented entrepreneurs. Participants gain practical skills to take their business to the next level, with topics such as financial statements, negotiations and marketing. Participants develop an actionable growth plan for the business with the help of business advisors and like-minded entrepreneurs. The Goldman Sachs program is free for participants—men and women—and delivered in partnership with academic institutions across the country. Learn more about eligibility and how to apply at www.10ksbapply.com.

The **Black-Owned Business Center**, created in partnership with Hello Alice and the NAACP, is offering more than $4 million in grants as part of a long-range commitment to advancing Black-owned small businesses. Individual grants range from $10,000 to $25,000. In addition to funding opportunities, all grant applicants will have access to the resources on Hello Alice, which include small business how-to guides, mentoring, digital support communities and additional funding opportunities. To apply for the grant series and to access resources, visit https://blackbiz.helloalice.com.

The **Tory Burch Foundation** offers fellowships to women entrepreneurs seeking to hone skills and grow their business. Annually, the program offers up to 50 women a one-year fellowship. It includes education, workshops and business guidance; a grant for business education; access to a private online peer community; and a trip to Tory Burch offices, among other benefits. The fellowship program typically accepts applications from late September until mid-November. For more information, visit www.toryburchfoundation.org.

Point Foundation provides scholarships, mentorship, leadership development and community service training for lesbian, gay, bisexual, transgender and queer students. The online application period for the scholarships generally runs from November through January each year. For more information or to apply, visit https://pointfoundation.org.

MENTAL AND PHYSICAL HEALTH

What happens if you get stuck with a big hospital bill you simply can't pay? As a first stop, you should try to work out payments with the billing department. Many medical centers have financial assistance programs—as well as connections to charities that can lend a financial hand—to help patients. But how do you find the care you need in tough times? The federal government may be the obvious place to look, but you'll also find nonprofits and industry groups that can help.

Medicare

If you are on Medicare and have trouble affording your premiums, you may be able to get help from your state. For information on Medicare Savings Programs and state contacts, visit www.medicare.gov, and search for "Medicare Savings Programs."

Medicaid

Funded jointly by the federal government and the states, Medicaid is a public insurance program that provides health coverage to people with low income, "including children, parents, pregnant women, seniors and people with disabilities," according to the Center on Budget and Policy Priorities. "Each state operates its own Medicaid program within federal guidelines."

For information on eligibility and how to apply, you can visit the website www.medicaid.gov and click "Learn How to Apply for Coverage" in the "About Us" section. In addition, Medicaid may be available to those who cannot afford to pay for long-term care.

Other Resources

Planned Parenthood Federation of America provides a wide range of services for women, men and young people, including general care, contraception, abortion services and referrals, cancer screening, testing and treatment of sexually transmitted infections, transgender health services and more. Digital tools include a free Spot On Period Tracker, a Roo chatbot answering questions about sexuality and relationships and a Chat/Text service staffed by sex educators. Find a health center online at www.plannedparenthood.org /health-center, or call 1-800-230-PLAN.

Medicine Assistance Tool (MAT). If you're struggling to afford your prescription medicines, many major pharmaceutical companies have patient-assistance programs that may be able to help with your copays or deductibles (if you have insurance) or supply free medications, depending on the case. For help finding programs, check the MAT's search engine at www.medicineassistancetool.org, operated by the trade group Pharmaceutical Research and Manufacturers of America (PhRMA). On that tool, you enter your list of medications, provide some personal information and then receive a list of prescription-assistance programs that may be available to you.

The nonprofit **NeedyMeds** offers a free source of information as well as assistance for people who are uninsured or underinsured and cannot afford their health care and medicines. It has information on more than 30,000 programs. NeedyMeds helps you locate free and low-cost medical, dental and mental health treatment and help paying medical transportation costs and other health care expenses. Its free NeedyMeds Drug Discount Card helps you save on prescription medicines if you are not using insurance, and its drug pricing calculator lets you compare drug costs at participating pharmacies in your area. You can access NeedyMeds' services through its website, www .needymeds.org, or its toll-free helpline, 800-503-6897.

National Alliance on Mental Illness. If you or a loved one struggle with a mental health issue, NAMI's resources may be able to help. The nonprofit NAMI provides an array of mental health resources, including education, support groups, the NAMI Helpline, online discussion groups and publications. Its free, peer-led support groups include the NAMI Connection for adults with a mental health condition and the NAMI Family Support groups for adults with a loved one with a mental health issue. Visit www.nami.org to locate your nearest NAMI Connection or Family Support group.

For mental health information, referrals and support, call the free NAMI Helpline at 1-800-950-NAMI Monday through Friday, from 10 a.m. to 6 p.m., Eastern Time (email: info@nami.org). For crisis situations, text "NAMI" to 741-741 for 24/7 support via text message from a trained crisis counselor.

16

HOW SOCIETY CAN— AND SHOULD—HELP

If you're like many single women in America, you're not having it easy and you could sure use some help.

If you're the "typical" woman, you're not getting paid as much as men—even though your rent isn't lower than a man's is for the same space, and your food items aren't cheaper. And if you're unwed, you're likely surviving on one income.

If you're a single mom with family to support, your salary has to stretch further. But with children, it's tougher to work overtime or take a second job to boost income. And childcare can be costly.

At times, you may feel as though you're fighting gravity as you strive to get ahead.

Mia Taylor, a single mother and head of household in San Diego, knows the story. Luckily, in the fall of 2020, her full-time job enabled her to work from home. But this cancer survivor is "constantly living on credit cards" to pay basic, daily expenses and limiting her food bill to $150 a week. In 2020, she bought sneakers for the first time in seven years.

The high cost of childcare has limited her access to jobs with better pay. Not long ago, she had been a finalist for a dream job that re-quired working outside her home, nine-to-five, five days a week. Her third interview was going well until the issue of salary arose. When Mia cited a figure that included the cost of childcare she'd need to take the job, the interview soon ended. Mia's requirement that the salary cover childcare had cost her the job.

What's wrong with this? Why should women be facing such obstacles to their career and self-support? And why are these problems allowed to persist?

Many of the reasons stem from age-old attitudes about women and their roles.

Traditionally, women have been expected to marry, have children and quit their jobs. In the workplace, this perception—this view that female employees were temporary—has been a license to discriminate: to limit women's job opportunities and pay.

And although various markers of these practices exist, one glaring example is the gender wage gap. It's a disparity that affects women's standard of living. And it's a sobering measure of how much society values the work women do.

As defined, the gender wage gap reflects the difference between men's and women's median earnings. It shows that even decades after the passage of such laws as the Equal Pay Act of 1963 and the Lilly Ledbetter Fair Pay Act of 2009, and a narrowing of the pay gap over time, women's wages overall still fall woefully short, compared with those of men. Consider: in 2019, the median usual weekly earnings of full-time wage and salary workers of women overall came to an annual average about 82 cents for every dollar earned by men, as US Bureau of Labor Statistics data show. For single women, the comparable figure was an even lower 73 cents.

This gender pay gap widens over a woman's career. And it can result in big losses in earnings opportunities. An October 2020 report by the National Women's Law Center (NWLC) states that "based on today's wage gap, a woman who works full-time, year-round, stands to lose $406,280 over a 40-year career."[1]

So eliminating the gender wage gap would be a milestone. Not only would it boost the financial security of women—especially for those managing on one income—but it would also help affirm the value of work women do.

That this hasn't happened already is hard to fathom. "It's astounding that the pay gap persists even now in this era of enlightenment about genders," says Riché Richardson, associate professor of African American literature at Cornell University. "The implication is that women's work and time are not as valuable as men's, and women's contributions are taken for granted."

But evidently, entrenched attitudes have been hard to change. And the wage gap has deep roots. "The gender pay gap is grounded in the history of patriarchy and the way women's labor has been valued," holds Zoe Spencer, professor of sociology at Virginia State University. "It's been men who have been able to assess what is valuable and assign a value to labor. For a long time, it was frowned upon for women to work. So, after World War II, when rising numbers of women did enter the workforce, their work was devalued." But Black women, she points out, "have always been in the workforce, providing free and, later, underpaid labor in segregated labor pools."

In the workplace, men have traditionally hired men for top positions, while women have been steered to lower-level service-type jobs—positions with limited pay and potential for advancement. In addition, working women with children have faced the "mommy penalty": that's the bias in which mothers could be paid less than, say, childless female colleagues, experts say, because employers have viewed working mothers as less committed to their jobs.

In a 2021 report, the National Partnership for Women and Families captured the essence of the wage gap this way: "Compared to men, women tend to hold lower-paying jobs, work in lower-paying industries, and spend less time in the formal workforce. These trends result from factors ranging from pervasive stereotypes and social norms about gender and work, to a lack of workplace support for family caregiving, to gender and racial discrimination, to the devaluation of work when it is primarily done by women—and the effects are both starker and qualitatively different for women of color."[2]

Certainly, the problem is bad enough for married working women in dual-income households. But it's that much worse for single women surviving on one income.

CORRECTING THE PROBLEMS

So the gender wage gap has to go. But how? How can society, which created the framework for a gender pay gap, reverse course? Instead of devaluing women workers, how should it expand women's career opportunities, helping women become scientists, medical practitioners, financiers or any other career options with a promising future? And how should it eradicate barriers to achievement, such as unaffordable education, or day care for family members that's priced out of reach?

Eliminating the obstacles to achievement of these goals requires broad cooperation. Homes and schools need to lay the groundwork by instilling confidence in children—girls as well as boys—that they can aim high and become what they wish, while government and business need to ensure economic opportunity through their laws and practices.

Growing up, Cornell's Riché Richardson was lucky. She got enlightened messages about women's roles from her grandmother, at home. "In school, girls were expected to do tasks. such as washing the blackboard," the future professor recalls. "But my grandmother told me not to do that. She said, 'You go to school to learn. You're not a maid.'" By following her grandmother's directive, "I couldn't get into teachers' good graces by washing the board. That meant I had to prove myself in the classroom."

EDUCATION

But too often, homes and schools haven't been sources of enlightenment about women's roles. As some experts explain, traditionally, boys more than girls have been encouraged to favor math and the sciences, while girls often have been steered toward socially minded subjects and the arts. One result has been the limited ranks of women in some well-paying, knowledge-based, careers.

Today, "women are only 28 percent of the workforce in STEM [science, technology, engineering and mathematics] fields, with particular gaps in computer sciences, technology and engineering," says

Kimberly Churches, chief executive officer at the American Association of University Women (AAUW). To help correct that imbalance, "we need practices, starting as early as pre-kindergarten, and lasting through high school, to ensure more young women pursue careers in STEM—which would set them up for a stronger financial future."

Beyond high school, higher education and/or training programs provide pathways to lucrative careers. But costs, especially at private colleges and universities, can be prohibitive. Options for reducing costs can range widely from expanding Pell grants for low-income students to forgiving some amount of student loans.

But lowering college costs is paramount. Having community colleges free for everyone "is a game changer. It creates a talent pool of more educated, local citizens, which is attractive to employers," points out Kimberly Churches of AAUW. Moreover, expanding the free options at four-year colleges and universities addresses national concerns: enabling more students to afford four years of higher education while reducing the student debt crisis.

There's also a pressing need for childcare. Today, many colleges provide this service to their professors. Given the rising number of nontraditional students—including single parents—colleges should make affordable childcare available to their students with children. "Even if tuition is free," the AAUW executive notes, "a single parent would be unable to attend classes if she couldn't afford care for minor children."

To be sure, investing in education can pay off socially and economically. Schooling can shape long-term attitudes and be a gateway to a fruitful career.

WORK

However, in the workplace, other issues come to the fore. Once on the job, women can continue to face obstacles ranging from unfair pay and barriers to promotions to outright sexual harassment. And although a growing number of laws and corporate policies address these issues today, the persistent gender wage gap underscores how much more effort is needed.

And as for working mothers? A 2020 report by the National Women's Law Center (NWLC) spells out problems they've faced: "Employers' negative stereotypes about mothers harm (their) job and salary prospects. In comparing equally qualified women candidates, one study revealed that mothers were recommended for significantly lower starting salaries, were perceived as less competent, and were less likely to be recommended for hire than non-mothers." But for dads, the opposite occurred: "Fathers were recommended for significantly higher pay and were perceived as more committed to their jobs than men without children."[3]

Beyond childcare, assisting elderly parents can take a toll on earnings and careers. The potential impact on single women: according to data in a 2020 report by the National Committee to Preserve Social Security and Medicare, "One example of the cumulative impact of the economic effects of caregiving is that single females caring for their elderly parents are 2.5 times more likely than non-caregivers to live in poverty in old age."[4]

EMPLOYMENT POLICIES

Thus, urgent action is needed. Given the depth of the wage gap problem, and its implications, eliminating it requires not only enlightened attitudes but also new rules (and better enforcement of existing ones).

There's been no shortage of proposals for change. Measures that would help close the wage gap have come from inside and outside of government and have ranged from national policies to specific employer practices. Among the common national themes: raising the minimum wage; boosting pay and benefits for those working in the traditionally lower-paying "women's jobs"; adopting permanent, national paid family leave and medical leave policies; better enforcing antidiscrimination regulations; better assisting families with the cost of childcare and other forms of family care and helping lower the costs of attending public colleges and universities.

In the workplace, calls for change involve a range of hiring and pay practices. Among them: publishing salary ranges for each job, prohibiting use of job candidates' salary history as a guide to hiring and wage determination and banning punishment of workers who discuss their wages with colleagues.

At the same time, more women need to fill leadership positions—evidently for the good of the organization as well as for women.

A report by McKinsey & Company shows how diversifying the ranks of corporate leadership pays off for business. And the benefits appear to be ongoing. As the May 2020 report states, "Our latest analysis reaffirms the strong business case for both gender diversity and ethnic and cultural diversity in corporate leadership, and shows that the business case continues to strengthen."[5]

As for gender diversity: McKinsey's 2019 analysis finds "that companies in the top quartile of gender diversity on executive teams were 25 percent more likely to experience above-average profitability than peer companies in the fourth quartile. This is up from 21 percent in 2017 and 15 percent in 2014." Moreover, the "higher the representation" (of women executives), noted the McKinsey report, "the higher the likelihood of outperformance."[6]

LEGISLATION

Hopefully, such findings will result in more women in (well-paying) leadership roles. But without any such guarantees, women need additional legislation—new, stronger equal pay laws that take up where earlier versions left off. As the AAUW has pointed out, "Nearly every state has a law prohibiting employers from paying workers differently based solely on their gender. But many of these laws are limited in scope or are not enforced. . . . [Thus] every state has room to make its pay equity laws stronger."[7]

On the federal level, the Paycheck Fairness Act is one of the proposals touted by many women's rights advocates. Introduced various times in Congress since 1997, the bill was proposed again in 2021 by Senator Patty Murray and Representative Rosa DeLauro. In April 2021 the bill passed in the US House of Representatives but two months later failed in the Senate.

The Paycheck Fairness Act would attack wage discrimination from numerous angles. It calls for banning retaliation against employees who discuss their salary with each other, limiting how employers can use job candidates' salary history in making hiring and wage decisions, mandating that employers be able to prove that pay disparities are due to legitimate job reasons and not gender, easing workers' ability to participate in class action lawsuits that charge systemic pay discrimination, creating a negotiation and skills training program for women and girls and improving the Department of Labor's tools for enforcing the Equal Pay Act.

But pay isn't the only form of discrimination. Beyond erasing the wage gap, employers need to eliminate biases in hiring and promotion. And they need to demonstrate equality and inclusion in their hiring practices.

FAMILY CARE

For working mothers, the cost and availability of childcare were critical problems well before the coronavirus tore through the globe in 2020. But the effects of this pandemic—the lockdowns, recession, job losses and the closures of schools and day care centers—were a disaster for many single moms. And they underscored the impact childcare can have on women's careers.

In its September 2020 Monthly Labor Review, the Bureau of Labor Statistics provided this grim assessment: "The current economic downturn resulting from the COVID-19 pandemic is disproportionately hurting women's employment, with ramifications that could be long lasting." The report's authors estimated that "15 million single mothers in the United States will be the most severely affected, with little potential for receiving other sources of childcare and a smaller likelihood of continuing to work during the crisis."

As an upside, the crisis did shine floodlights on the need for reforms to the childcare system, including its cost and availability.

In fact, some in Congress had been eyeing childcare problems before the coronavirus struck. In one notable example, Senator Patty Murray and Representative Bobby Scott introduced the Child Care for Working Families Act in 2017 and reintroduced it two years later. The bill addresses a host of childcare concerns, from more affordable, quality care options that parents need for their kids to better pay and training for childcare workers. The bill was reintroduced in 2021.

Moreover, after his inauguration, President Joe Biden moved quickly to address childcare issues: signed into law in March 2021, his $1.9 trillion coronavirus relief package, called the American Rescue Plan, included major expansions to the Child Tax Credit and the Child and Dependent Care Tax Credit (see chapter 10).

RETIREMENT

But what about retired single women—those who have relied on their own income but have earned less than men during their working years? Will many have to struggle in old age? Will their money last?

These concerns can plague women, especially if they live alone. Of course, having savings helps immeasurably. But for many single women, saving money during their working years is a strain; it's potentially impossible if their wages are low.

And even if they have accumulated assets, life events can take a toll. As part of a divorce settlement, for instance, ex-spouses can end up with sharply lower assets than they'd shared as a married couple. If their breakup occurs later in life, divorcées have less time to replenish lost assets, points out Tyler Bond, research manager at the National Institute on Retirement Security (NIRS). And widows, he notes, may be left with high health care costs if a spouse suffered a long illness before dying. Paying those expenses could drain the savings the spouse's widow would have inherited.

Of course, many seniors rely on Social Security. Indeed, among elderly Social Security beneficiaries, 70 percent of unmarried persons receive 50 percent or more of their income from their monthly checks, reports the Social Security Administration. Thus, improving benefits of this financial bedrock would be a boon, especially to single women: their overall lifetime earnings, which are typically less than men's, produce a lower Social Security benefit.

Among the proposals to enhance Social Security's benefits: increasing the minimum benefit and the cost-of-living adjustment, providing Social Security credits to individuals who leave the workforce to care for needy family members and improving the benefits for certain widows and widowers.

If adopted, such changes could be especially vital to women. But what's the outlook? Will America step up and address the financial inequities facing women, especially singles? Will society finally grasp the ways single women get financially left behind?

So far, the signs haven't been promising: the needs of single women haven't gained traction in today's family-focused society.

Thus it's time to balance the financial scales. America needs to scrap the traditional attitudes and discriminatory practices that economically harm women—especially singles. Families, schools and public and private institutions all need to respond to this call for economic justice. America's 66 million single women deserve nothing less.

NOTES

CHAPTER 1

1. Allianz Life Insurance Company of North America, *Allianz, Women, Money, and Power: Discoveries for Women, Money and Power White Paper 2006*, 11, https://www.allianzlife.com/-/media/files/allianz/documents/ent _277_n_wmp_2006_white_paper.pdf.

2. Caring.com, "2021 Wills and Estate Planning Study," https://www.caring .com/caregivers/estate-planning/wills-survey.

CHAPTER 2

1. Fidelity Investments, "Single Women & Money Study," November 2017, https://newsroom.fidelity.com/press-releases/news-details/2017/Single -Women-on-the-Rise-but-Too-Often-Missing-Key-Opportunities-to-Safe guard-their-Futures/default.aspx.

2. Fidelity Investments, "Engine Group Caravan Survey," June 6–8, 2019, email, 2020.

3. Allianz Life Insurance Company of North America, "2019 Women, Money & Power Study Summary Sheet," June 2019, 2, https://www.allianz life.com/-/media/files/allianz/pdfs/newsroom/2019-women-money-and -power-summary-sheet.pdf.

4. Merrill Lynch and Age Wave, "Widowhood and Money: Resiliency, Responsibility and Empowerment," 2018, https://agewave.com/what-we-do /landmark-research-and-consulting/research-studies/widowhood-lifestage -from-honoring-the-past-to-moving-forward.

CHAPTER 3

1. US Bureau of Labor Statistics, "Consumer Units of Single Females by Age of Reference Person: Average Annual Expenditures and Characteristics, Consumer Expenditure Survey, 2018–2019," Table 4110, September 2020, https://www.bls.gov/cex/2019/CrossTabs/singlesbyage/femalage.PDF.

2. National Association of Realtors, *2020 Profile of Home Buyers and Sellers*, November 2020, 37, https://www.nar.realtor.

3. Ibid., 96.

4. National Association of Personal Financial Advisors, "The State of Financial Planning in America," January 2020, https://www.napfa.org/the-state-of -financial-planning-in-america.

CHAPTER 4

1. Moms Rising, "On Moms' Equal Pay Day, We Honor and Demand Action for Black Moms Who Experience Multiple Forms of Oppression Inside and Outside the Workplace," June 4, 2020, https://www.momsrising.org /newsroom/on-moms-equal-pay-day-we-honor-and-demand-action-for-black -moms-who-experience-multiple.

2. Yuliya Babushkina, *Hidden Currents: Under-the-Surface Changes in the Employee Benefits Market*, 2018, 10, 11, LIMRA, https://www.limra .com/contentassets/15b05e49b50a49f9b53edff187d6d058/180131-01.pdf ?research_id=10737454836.

3. Child Care Aware of America, "Picking Up the Pieces: Building a Better Child Care System Post COVID-19," Fall 2020, https://www.childcare aware.org/picking-up-the-pieces.

4. Ibid.

5. Rasheed Malik, "Working Families Are Spending Big Money on Child Care," Center for American Progress, June 20, 2019, https://www.american progress.org/issues/early-childhood/reports/2019/06/20/471141/working -families-spending-big-money-child-care.

6. Ibid.

CHAPTER 5

1. National Women's Law Center, "The Wage Gap: The Who, How, Why and What to Do," October 2020 factsheet, https://nwlc.org/wp-content/up loads/2019/09/Wage-Gap-Who-how.pdf.

2. Bonnie Marcus, *Not Done Yet! How Women over 50 Regain Their Confidence and Claim Workplace Power* (Vancouver, Canada: Page Two Books, 2021).

3. Joni Hersch and Jennifer Bennett Shinall, "Something to Talk About: Information Exchange under Employment Law," *University of Pennsylvania Law Review* 49 (2016), https://scholarship.law.vanderbilt.edu/faculty-publi cations/665.

CHAPTER 6

1. Jacqueline DeMarco, "Study: More than 1 in 3 Credit Cardholders Ending 2019 with More Credit Card Debt than They Started With," Lendingtree, December 23, 2019, https://www.lendingtree.com/credit-cards/study /cardholders-ending-2019-more-card-debt/#gender.

2. Geng Li, "Gender-Related Differences in Credit Use and Credit Scores," *FEDS Notes*, June 22, 2018, https://doi.org/10.17016/2380-7172.2188.

3. Mary Griffin and Michele Scarborough, "Need Help with Your Credit Card Debt? Start with Your Credit Card Company!" *Consumer Financial Protection Bureau* (blog), April 3, 2019, https://www.consumerfinance.gov/about -us/blog/need-help-your-credit-card-debt-start-your-credit-card-company.

4. Consumer Financial Protection Bureau, "What Are Debt Settlement/ Debt Relief Services and Should I Use Them?" February 15, 2017, https:// www.consumerfinance.gov/ask-cfpb/what-are-debt-settlementdebt-relief -services-and-should-i-use-them-en-1457.

5. Adam Looney, David Wessel and Kadija Yilla, "Who Owes All That Student Debt? And Who'd Benefit if It Were Forgiven?" Brookings Institution, January 28, 2020, https://www.brookings.edu/policy2020/votervital/who -owes-all-that-student-debt-and-whod-benefit-if-it-were-forgiven.

CHAPTER 7

1. Brad M. Barber and Terrance Odean, "Boys Will Be Boys: Gender, Overconfidence, and Common Stock Investment," *Quarterly Journal of Economics*, February 2001.

2. "Historical Returns on Stocks, Bonds, and Bills: 1926–2020," NYU Stern School of Business, January 2021, http://pages.stern.nyu.edu/~adamodar/New_Home_Page/datafile/histretSP.html.

3. Ben Johnson, "Morningstar's Active Passive Barometer: August 2020," Morningstar, https://www.morningstar.com/lp/active-passive-barometer.

CHAPTER 8

1. US SIF Foundation, *Report on US Sustainable and Impact Investing Trends 2020*, https://www.ussif.org/trends.

2. Sean Collins and Kristen Sullivan, "Advancing Environmental, Social, and Governance Investing," *Deloitte Insights*, Deloitte, February 20, 2020, https://www2.deloitte.com/content/dam/insights/us/articles/5073_Advancing-ESG-investing/DI_Advancing-ESG-investing_UK.pdf.

3. US SIF Foundation, *Report on US Sustainable and Impact Investing Trends 2020*.

4. MSCI, "MSCI KLD 400 Social Index (USD)," https://www.msci.com/documents/10199/904492e6-527e-4d64-9904-c710bf1533c6.

5. Ibid.

CHAPTER 9

1. Council for Disability Awareness, Chances of Disability webpage data, https://www.disabilitycanhappen.org/disability-statistic. Data based on Johanna Maleh and Tiffany Bosley, "Disability and Death Probability Tables for Insured Workers Born in 1997," Social Security Administration, October 2017.

2. Council for Disability Awareness, "10 Million Single Female Workers at Extreme Financial Risk from a Disability," June 2019, https://disabilitycanhappen.org/wp-content/uploads/2019/06/singlewomen_,mediakit.pdf#.

3. Scam Spotter, https://www.scamspotter.org.

CHAPTER 10

1. Scott Eastman, "How Many Taxpayers Itemize Under Current Law?" Tax Foundation, September 12, 2019, https://taxfoundation.org/standard-deduction-itemized-deductions-current-law-2019.

CHAPTER 11

1. Katherine Roy, Lori Lucas, Jack VanDerhei, Kelly Hahn, Je Oh and Livia Salonen, "The 3% Difference: What Leads to Higher Retirement Savings Rates?" J.P. Morgan, June 3, 2020, https://am.jpmorgan.com/us/en/asset-management/institutional/insights/retirement-insights/the-3-differ ence-what-leads-to-higher-retirement-savings-rates.

2. Georgetown University, McCourt School of Public Policy, Center for Retirement Initiatives, "State Initiatives 2021: More New Programs to Launch While Others Consider Action," accessed February 2, 2021, https:// cri.georgetown.edu/states.

CHAPTER 12

1. Social Security Administration, "What Every Woman Should Know," Publication 05-10127, July 2020, https://www.ssa.gov/pubs/EN-05-10127 .pdf.

2. Social Security Administration, "Social Security Is Important to Women," Factsheet, July 2019, https://www.ssa.gov/news/press/factsheets /women-alt.pdf.

3. Benjamin Veghte, "Social Security's Past, Present and Future," National Academy of Social Insurance, August 13, 2015, https://www.nasi.org /discuss/2015/08/social-security percentE2 percent80 percent99s-past-pres ent-future.

4. Kathleen Romig, "Social Security Lifts More Americans above Poverty than Any Other Program," Center on Budget and Policy Priorities, February 20, 2020, https://www.cbpp.org/research/social-security/social-security-lifts -more-americans-above-poverty-than-any-other-program.

5. Social Security Administration, "Historical Background and Development of Social Security," https://www.ssa.gov/history/briefhistory3.html.

6. C. Eugene Steuerle and Caleb Quackenbush, "Social Security and Medicare Lifetime Benefits and Taxes," Publication 66116/2000378, Urban Institute, September 2015, https://www.urban.org/sites/default/files /publication/66116/2000378-Social-Security-and-Medicare-Lifetime -Benefits-and-Taxes.pdf.

7. Social Security Administration, "Fast Facts & Figures about Social Security, 2020," Publication 13-11785, July 2020, https://www.ssa.gov/policy /docs/chartbooks/fast_facts/index.html.

8. Social Security Administration, "A Summary of the 2020 Annual Reports," Social Security and Medicare Board of Trustees, https://www.ssa.gov/oact/TRSUM.

9. Kathleen Romig, "Social Security Lifts More Americans above Poverty than Any Other Program."

10. Nationwide Retirement Institute Annual Survey, 2018, https://www.nationwide.com.

11. Social Security Administration, "The Faces and Facts of Disability," https://www.ssa.gov/disabilityfacts/facts.html.

12. Social Security Administration, "Disabled Worker Beneficiary Statistics by Calendar Year, Quarter, and Month," https://www.ssa.gov/oact/STATS/dibStat.html.

13. America's Health Insurance Plans, "State of Medigap 2020," https://www.ahip.org/research.

CHAPTER 13

1. "The Allianz Women, Power, and Money® Study: Empowered and Underserved," Allianz Life Insurance Company of North America, ENT-1462-N, 2012.

2. William P. Bengen, "Determining Withdrawal Rates Using Historical Data," *Journal of Financial Planning*, October 1994, 14–24, https://www.retailinvestor.org/pdf/Bengen1.pdf.

CHAPTER 14

1. Federal Interagency Forum on Aging-Related Statistics, "Older Americans 2020: Key Indicators of Well-Being," https://agingstats.gov/data.html.

2. Joanne Binette and Kerri Vasold, "2018 Home and Community Preferences: A National Survey of Adults Ages 18-Plus," AARP Research, August 2018, revised July 2019, https://www.aarp.org/research/topics/community/info-2018/2018-home-community-preference.html.

3. Genworth, "Cost of Care Survey," last accessed February 15, 2021, https://www.genworth.com/aging-and-you/finances/cost-of-care.html.

4. CARF International, "Consumer Guide to Understanding Financial Performance & Reporting in Continuing Care Retirement Communities," June 2016, http://www.carf.org/Resources/RetirementLiving.

5. Genworth LTC Insurance Calculator, last accessed February 15, 2021, https://www.genworth.com/products/care-funding/long-term-care-insurance /ltc-insurance-calculator.html.

6. Donald Redfoot, Lynn Feinberg, and Ari Houser, "The Aging of the Baby Boom and the Growing Care Gap: A Look at Future Declines in the Availability of Family Caregivers," AARP Public Policy Institute, *Insight on the Issues*, no. 85, August 2013.

CHAPTER 16

1. National Women's Law Center, "The Wage Gap: The Who, How, Why, and What to Do," October 2020, https://www.nwlc.org/wp-content /uploads/2019/09/Wage-Gap-Who-how.pdf.

2. National Partnership for Women and Families, "America's Women and the Wage Gap," *Fact Sheet*, March 2021, 3, https://www.nationalpartnership .org/our-work/resources/economic-justice/fair-pay/americas-women-and -the-wage-gap.pdf.

3. National Women's Law Center, "The Wage Gap: The Who, How, Why, and What to Do," October 2020 Fact Sheet, https://nwlc.org/wp-content /uploads/2019/09/Wage-Gap-Who-how.pdf. That report references a study by Shelley J. Correll, Stephen Benard and In Paik, "Getting a Job: Is There a Motherhood Penalty?" *American Journal of Sociology* 112 (March 2007): 1297–1338.

4. National Committee to Preserve Social Security and Medicare, "Women and Retirement: The Gender Gap Persists," August 2020, https:// www.ncpssm.org/eleanors-hope2__trashed/issue-briefs__trashed/women -and-retirement-the-gender-gap-persists.

5. Sundiatu Dixon-Fyle, Kevin Dolan, Vivian Hunt and Sara Prince, "Diversity Wins: How Inclusion Matters," McKinsey & Company, May 2020, 3, https://www.mckinsey.com/featured-insights/diversity-and-inclusion/diver sity-wins-how-inclusion-matters#.

6. Ibid.

7. American Association of University Women, "The Simple Truth about the Gender Pay Gap, 2020 Update, the Impact of COVID-19 on Women's Economic Security," 6, https://www.aauw.org/app/uploads/2020/12/Simple Truth_2.1.pdf.

INDEX

Page numbers in *italics* refer to figures and tables.

ABOUT THE AUTHORS

Margaret Price is an author, editor and journalist. She has been an editor at *Bloomberg Wealth Manager* magazine, international editor at Crain Communications' *Pensions & Investments* publication and senior editor at *Treasury & Risk Management* magazine. She also has written for such prominent publications as *Investor's Business Daily*, *New York Daily News*, *Newsday* newspaper and the *Christian Science Monitor*. Price is a member and past president of the New York Financial Writers' Association. She also is the author of the book *Emerging Stock Markets: A Complete Investment Guide to New Markets around the World*. Active in her community, she is cochair of the Women and Families Committee of Community Board 8–Manhattan. Price is a 2021 recipient of a New York State Women of Distinction award, presented by State Assembly Member Rebecca Seawright.

Jill Gianola is a published author and teacher and the founder of Gianola Financial Planning, a fee-only planning firm. Her work has been recognized by *Mutual Funds* magazine, which named her one of the top 100 planners in the United States, and *Money* magazine, which featured her advice in "Secrets of America's Top Advisors." She is the author of *The Young Couple's Guide to Growing Rich Together*, named "one of 10 books you should read if you want to retire rich," by the Insider website. She has written personal finance columns for the iVillage website and *All You* magazine. She has taught personal finance courses at Ohio State University, Franklin University and Columbus State Community College, and economics at Wittenberg University.